LITTLE GIRLS LOST

EILEEN ORMSBY

In memory of Shauna Howe, Sian Kingi, Leigh Leigh and Martha Puebla

CONTENTS

WHAT CRITICS HAVE SAID

"Ormsby has delivered a triumph of narrative journalism, meticulously researched and gripping, a skilful mergence of tech jargon with human drama." *The Saturday Paper*

"The book is a fascinating expose of this particular aspect of the "dark web" of internet dealings and its subsequent unravelling." *Sydney Morning Herald*

"Ormsby's investigative journalism shines as she provides a very thorough account of Ulbricht's rise and fall." *Penthouse Magazine*

"What pulls you through The Darkest Web isn't its often-nefarious, sometimes-gory details, but Ormsby's handling of three progressively intense narrative arcs." *The Guardian*

"The darkness has become a repository for human cruelty, perversion and psychosis, and Ormsby captures all the tragedy in her gripping book." *The Australian*

"A great strength of the meticulously researched Silk Road is the manner in which Ormsby gently takes the reader by the hand, unpacking the technology underpinning this 'dark net' market." *Australian Police Journal*

"A disillusioned corporate lawyer turned writer from Australia, Eileen's new book, The Darkest Web, is the story of her journey, from drug markets and contract killing sites to the Internet's seediest alcoves. But the most startling moments of the book happen when she comes face-to-face with some of its key players." *VICE*

"From the Internet's hidden drug dens to torture-porn websites, Ormsby has seen it all. If you've ever wondered what the Dark Web is really like, Darkest Web should be on your TBR." *Bustle Magazine: The Best New True Crime Books You Can Read Right Now*

"Riveting." *Who Magazine*

"Investigative journalism that gallops along at a cracking pace." *SMH Good Weekend*

"Through her clear rendering of the facts, Ormsby makes the intricacies of the technology involved accessible to even the most technophobic of readers. The tone is conversational and friendly while the content is intriguing and increasingly dark. In her quest to uncover the mystery behind the enigmatic DPR she uncovers a story of subterfuge, replete with conspiracy theories and hidden identities, that is rich with anecdotes." *Newtown Review of Books*

"Ormsby is a great writer, giving us gripping accounts from the people who actually used "Silk Road" to paint an accurate picture of how the website was created, run, and ultimately fell . . . Silk Road is easily one of the best books I've read this year." *The Library NZ*

"Silk Road is one of the more readable and gripping true crime books of recent times. It is not just Ormsby's knowledge of the brief but spectacular rise and fall of Silk Road that makes for compelling reading, but also the ordering of the material so that the reader has the sense of being educated in the technical and legal background to an astonishing criminal enterprise." *The Australian*

"For the most complete account of the original Silk Road ... Eileen Ormsby's book Silk Road is the best place to start. It's full of original research, interviews and insight. This is best read along with her excellent blog, AllThingsVice, which covers several aspects of the dark net, but especially the dark net markets." *Jamie Bartlett, author of Darknet and Radicals*

"[*Stalkers* is] chilling... harrowing...unpicks the sordid tale from the start" *The Sun*

"Dark, disturbing and near unbelievable... [*Stalkers* is] my No.1 true crime read this year" *OzNoir*

ABOUT THE AUTHOR

Eileen Ormsby is a lawyer, author and freelance journalist based in Melbourne, Australia. Her first book, *Silk Road*, was the world's first in-depth expose of the black markets that operate on the dark web. In *The Darkest Web*, Eileen's gonzo-style investigations led her deep into the secretive corners of the dark web where drugs and weapons dealers, hackers, hitmen and worse ply their trade. Many of these dark web interactions turned into real-world relationships, entanglements, hack attempts on her computer and even death threats from the dark web's most successful hitman network.

Eileen started writing scripts for *Casefile True Crime Podcast* in 2018 and has since become one of the show's most regular contributors. She often focuses on cases that have a dark web or internet aspect to them.

Connect with Eileen via social media by clicking an icon below. She is most active on Twitter

INTRODUCTION

Some of the stories in this book contain references to
sexual violence committed against children. Reader
discretion is advised.

Every parent knows the horrific feeling when a toddler
goes missing for just a few minutes. *They were right here. I
looked away for two seconds. Where could they have gone?
What if....*

The same feeling returns in later years, when a child
is late returning home, especially if there is no way to
contact them. In 99% of cases, this sick feeling comes to
an abrupt halt when the toddler is spotted making a
beeline toward an amusement ride or the older child
comes home with tales of a bus missed or losing track of
time because of the fun they were having. Sharp words
may be spoken as the tension is replaced by annoyance at

having been made to feel that way, but the overwhelming emotion is relief.

Imagine the horror of that feeling for those parents for whom there is no happy ending. The increasing anxiety and terror as the minutes turn into hours, then days, only to culminate in every parent's worst nightmare. Rather than being reunited with an errant child, the parents are called to identify a body.

Few things arouse the emotions and engender such outrage as the murder of a child. It is not uncommon to see people reacting to brutality against a child with calls for the death penalty, or worse, for the perpetrator. The reaction is visceral, the need to protect primal.

The murder of pre-teen and teenage girls usually involves an element of sexual assault, and this is true in three of the four case studies in this book. A disturbing theme emerged during the research for these stories and others like them. When the victim is a pre-teen girl, there is an absolute belief in their innocence. But, when it comes to teenagers, a certain amount of victim-blaming sometimes enters the discourse. What was she wearing? How was she acting? What did she do to bring this upon herself? There are elements of these attitudes in both of the stories about teenagers in this book.

The stories in this book can broadly be placed into two categories: sexually motivated child abductions and teen-on-teen violence culminating in murder. The victims are all girls, aged from eleven to sixteen. None of them survived their ordeal. This book is not for everyone, so please take this as a content warning.

Sexually motivated child abductions

"The sudden and unprovoked nature of these attacks, the brutality of the offences, and the powerlessness and defencelessness of most of the victims combine to make these incidents amongst the most disturbing of all homicides."

— WALLACE A (1986). *HOMICIDE: THE SOCIAL REALITY*, NEW SOUTH WALES BUREAU OF CRIME STATISTICS AND RESEARCH, SYDNEY.

Parents since time immemorial have been terrified of that period when their daughter transitions from child to pre-teen to teenager, when she gains that little bit of independence and yearns to go out to explore the world for herself. The idea of predators waiting to harm our little girls can be paralyzing, but as parents we know we must allow them certain freedoms. A feeling of slight unease becomes an almost constant companion, not letting up until they are safely home, tucked up in bed and away from those who would wish them harm, at least until tomorrow.

Even though we know that the vast majority of harm that might come to a pre-teen or teenage girl will come from someone she knows, the fear of the one-in-a-million chance of a stranger abduction makes our desire to keep them close, to not allow them out after dark, more urgent. Nobody wants to live through every parent's nightmare— the violent loss of their child. It is not the natural order of things to outlive our children.

Abductions and murders involving children, and in particular those that involve sexual assault, generate intense media attention and widespread public concern, despite their infrequency. Even though there are hundreds of other harms that can come to our children that are far more likely to befall them, the idea of their final days, hours or minutes being spent in abject terror with a stranger doing unspeakable acts to them is unfathomable.

Those who kidnap children who are not known to them for the purposes of sexual abuse are most often male and Caucasian, offending within their own race. Psychological studies of sexually motivated murderers and their crimes have placed them into two broad categories—the "opportunistic–impulsive" offender and the "sadistic–calculator" offender.

The opportunistic–impulsive offender will often be known to the victim. The victim might be in a particularly vulnerable state—she may be drunk or walking alone late at night. The act itself is likely to be sudden, random and brutal, and the victim killed in order not to protect the identity of her attacker. The murder of Leigh Leigh, the third story in this book, falls within this archetype. Arguably, so does that of Shauna Howe, whose story is the first in this book.

The sadistic–calculator offender, on the other hand, is likely to choose his victim and approach her under a pretense that lowers her defenses. This type of offender is aroused by deliberate torture and the act is usually drawn out with the victim imprisoned, bound and beaten, the sexual assault containing elements of bondage. Upon death, the sadistic–calculator will conceal the victim's corpse and keep some sort of record or memento of the event. The infamous Australian case of the abduction, rape and murder of fourteen-year-old Lauren Margaret Barry and sixteen-year-old Nichole Emma Collins in 1997 (the "Bega schoolgirl case") was carried out by sexual sadist Leslie Alfred Camilleri and an accomplice who was said to be of low IQ and who was heavily influenced by the older man. The case bore chilling resemblances to that of Sian Kingi, whose story is the second in this book. She also had the misfortune to encounter a sadistic–calculator type of offender who also was assisted by someone, in this case, a woman who was desperate for his approval.

The decision by these offenders to attack a child could be because the offender is a pedophile, with a deviant sexual preference for children. However, just as often it is because a child represents an easy target, being physically weaker, vulnerable and more easily intimidated than an adult woman.

When abductions are committed by strangers, they can be extremely difficult to investigate. Police face the challenge of identifying an unknown person with no obvious ties to the victim, who has most likely left the immediate area where the abduction has taken place.

The type of person who would carry out such a heinous crime is a real life bogeyman. He epitomizes evil, which is why the newspapers are so keen to report his crimes. As most primary school–aged children are abducted close to their home, or somewhere else where they should be considered safe, there is an element of bad luck. It is something that could happen to any of our children, no matter how careful or blameless we might be. It is every parent's nightmare come true.

"Boys will be Boys"

> "The code of toxic masculinity requires that men are dominant over everyone else, have no needs, show no emotion and are always winning."
>
> — ELLEN HENDRIKSON, "HOW TO FIGHT TOXIC MASCULINITY" SCIENTIFIC AMERICAN (2019)

The third and fourth stories in this book involve teen-on-teen crime. One is sexually motivated, but the other does not have a sexual element to it at all. However, both cases have their roots in deep-seated toxic masculinity.

Toxic masculinity, of course, does not refer to all men or all forms of masculinity, but rather a specific (and increasingly outdated) notion of masculinity and what it means to be a man. Although society now has a much broader view of manhood, in the 1970s and 80s, especially in rural and regional areas, boys were taught from a very young age that showing any emotion was considered weak or feminine. "Real men" were tough, had no needs or feelings and took on traditional roles in the home. Any boy whose behavior fell outside the accepted masculinity was bullied and shunned. Unsurprisingly, such cultural lessons were often linked to aggression and violence in the boys and young men. As they turned into teenagers, aggressive masculinity often went hand-in-hand with participation in drinking rituals. Men—or even teenage boys—who didn't drink alcohol were to be distrusted or ridiculed.

Women and girls existed to fulfil certain roles and had worth only to the extent they filled those roles, whether "Madonna" (the sort of girl a "real man" would want to marry) or "whore" (the type of girl who could be used and discarded). The friendship and camaraderie among men was given precedence over any relationships with women—"bros before hoes" as the old saying goes.

With such a narrow and aggressive notion of what a man is, criminal conduct can be written off as understandable, a part of growing up, or just "boys being boys." When a sexual assault is involved, questions may be raised about how the woman (or girl) may have contributed to her rape or assault. Sometimes a community even supports the boys involved. They don't want to see the lives and careers of their town's sons ruined because of "a youthful mistake."

Although it would be nice to think that such attitudes are relics of the past, some recent cases illustrate that there is still some way to go. In January 2015, nineteen-year-old Brock Turner raped a fellow student when she was passed out drunk behind a dumpster. Although he was convicted, he was sentenced to just six months in prison. His family felt that penalty was too harsh. Brock's father told the court that his son's life had been ruined: "That is a steep price to pay for just twenty minutes of action out of twenty-plus years of his life." He did not even acknowledge the unconscious twenty-three-year-old who was raped and arguably had her life ruined somewhat more than the rapist. It was thanks to the victim's bravery and eloquence, and the powerful statement she read out in court about the impact the rape had in her life, that Brock Turner got the media attention he deserved, if not the prison sentence.

In domestic violence circumstances, this is known as the "good guy" fallacy. If a boy or man is popular, engaging and fun to be around, nobody wants to believe he is capable of a heinous and violent crime behind closed doors. There is a general consensus that rape is bad; however, in some circles there is a persistent belief that some rapes are not as bad as others. Sex workers have continuously faced judgment and barriers to reporting their rapes. They have famously been a group targeted by serial killers because there is the perception their murders will not be investigated as rigorously as others, as violence is a risk of the job.

When it comes to sexual assault, any victim who does not act within society's perception of how a girl "should" behave might find themselves coming under unfair scrutiny, especially if the accused is a "good guy." People will look at the behavior of the girl involved and ask what she did to bring this upon herself. A narrative may emerge that she had consented and then experienced day-after regret—that the rape never really happened at all. Everyone rallies around the girl who is dragged from the street by a stranger and attacked. But when the attack happens to a woman who wears revealing clothes or lives in a way that conservative society deems inappropriate, it is easy for people to rally behind the man, especially if they consider him to be more representative of them and their community.

When such attacks happen in small or tight-knit

communities, the victim may find herself the subject of scrutiny and blame. She may be encouraged not to report it—to put it behind her or the town will turn on her. She may become the object of a smear campaign, rumors, accusations of lying or malevolent intent, or even further assaults. Friends might turn away from her, afraid that they will become the next targets. Her family may also become the target of anger from those who would prefer to protect the town's sons than their daughters.

When a community is able to turn a sexual assault around to blame the victim, parents can tell themselves that it couldn't possibly happen to their family. Their daughter would never be promiscuous, drink too much, go to the wrong parties. It provides an illusion of control. Further, if they see some semblance of their son in the accused, it can provide some comfort if they convince themselves the victim put herself in that position, is exaggerating or outright lying.

Although these kinds of assaults don't usually end in murder, there can be devastating consequences for the victim. In 2012, fourteen-year-old Daisy Coleman was sexually assaulted at a house party. Her accused rapist later drove her home and left her lying on her front porch in a T-shirt and sweatpants, overnight in sub-zero temperatures. Her mother found her the next morning. It was so cold, her hair had frozen to the ground. A seventeen-year-old boy, a popular athlete at the school, was arrested, but charges were later dropped against him, as well as another boy who had filmed the attack on his cell phone.

As if the assault wasn't bad enough, Daisy and her family became the target of a relentless campaign of bullying in her hometown. Before the trial, she was accused of being a liar and given the favorite epithets of rapists, "slut" and "whore." Daisy's brother was taunted and told that the video of her assault was being passed around the boys at his school.

County Sheriff Darren White told reporters that Daisy's family ought to "get over it." He denied the existence of a video circulating the school, taking the word of the teenager who recorded the assault that he had immediately deleted the footage. The sheriff said in a Netflix special, "Without pointing fingers, it serves to benefit people's causes by making things up that really didn't happen and really doesn't exist. Don't underestimate the need for attention—especially young girls." Further victim-blaming was heaped on by a defense attorney who went on television to say, "What did she expect sneaking out of the house at 1.00 a.m.?"

When the Coleman family raised questions about the charges against the boy, whose family had strong political connections, being dropped, the local community turned on them and the bullying intensified. Daisy was blamed for the unwelcome media attention on the town and the school from the rest of the nation. Eventually the accused pleaded guilty to the misdemeanor charge of endangering the life of a child, for dumping Daisy outside when she was comatose. He received probation. The relentless attacks on Daisy and her family didn't ease up—if anything, they intensified. Their house was vandalized, threats were made against all members of the family, and eventually they had to leave the town.

Daisy became an outspoken activist for survivors of sexual assault, campaigning across the USA. In 2020, she died by her own hand at age twenty-three. Those who knew her said that the person she had the potential to become had really been killed on that cold night in 2012 at the age of fourteen.

At the very worst end of toxic masculinity is the participation in pack, or gang, rapes. Some rapists report a sense of camaraderie and bonding with their "mates" when carrying out a pack rape. They will often refer to their victims as "sluts" (regardless of past sexual history) who "deserved" or "were asking for it," especially if the victim is alcohol-affected, even if the offenders themselves had plied the victim with alcohol in the first place.

In 2012, two popular footballers from Steubenville High School carried an unconscious teenager from place to place, sexually assaulting her and filming their crimes. The young girl did not know she had been raped until the pictures started circulating on social media. Most of the town rallied behind the boys, blaming the "drunk slut" for ruining their athletic careers with her accusations. The victim and her family were shamed and shunned by the town. Some of the news reporters expressed sympathy for the boys who "had their lives ruined" by the accusations. It wasn't until the hacktivist (hacker–activist) group Anonymous intervened, as they had done earlier that year for Daisy Coleman, that public opinion slowly focused on the real victim of the crime and also revealed others who had been involved. More than a dozen people had posted photos and videos of the six-hour assault on Twitter, Facebook, Instagram and YouTube, that showed the sixteen-year old—clearly unconscious—being carried from place to place, sexually assaulted and urinated on.

The rapists were convicted, but both served less than two years in prison.

The third story in this book, that of Leigh Leigh, has many parallels to the Steubenville High case, but with an even more devastating outcome. Leigh's assault came thirty years earlier, in regional Australia—a time when toxic masculinity was the only kind and a place where men substantially outnumbered the women. Regional and remote areas have historically tended to be more homogeneous than metropolitan cities, less tolerant of those who are different, and more likely to prefer traditional gender roles.

This is exactly the environment that Leigh grew up in. What happened to her when she accepted an invitation to a high school party has become one of the greatest blights on one town's history. It is also a seminal case of victim-blaming, not just by the perpetrators and their supporters, but the media and court system as well.

Sadly, the narrative of the irresponsibly drunken girl versus the popular sports-playing "boys being boys" from "good families" continues to rear its head even in 2020. The horror that befell Leigh occurred in a time before cell phones, but there is little doubt that if it had happened today, vision of the assaults on her would have made it to social media.

The final case in this book is a departure from the others, as it does not involve a sexual assault. However, it does continue the theme of a teenage girl living in an environment of toxic masculinity—this time in the world of violent street gangs. Martha Puebla was badly let down by those who were supposed to protect her. She was a teenage girl used as a pawn in the games of men.

It is likely that most readers will have never heard of Martha Puebla, whose life was brutally cut short when she was just sixteen, even though the crime was extensively reported news and a popular documentary was made about it. That is because all of the publicity was focused on the man accused of her murder and the role that the sitcom *Curb Your Enthusiasm* played in the outcome. As a result, Martha's name has all but been forgotten.

Police response

> *Reality TV police perform a distorted, sanitised and more entertaining version of police work... The reality of reality TV is that it is unreal.*

— STEPHENSON, ANTONY. "POLICE AS TELEVISION VIEWERS AND POLICING PRACTITIONERS." *FUSION JOURNAL*, NO. 7, 2015.

The four stories in this book take place in different eras in different parts of the world, but all are accounts of young girls who had their lives snuffed out far too early through no fault of their own. Naturally, all of the stories involve an element of police investigation.

Most of us won't have first hand knowledge of how law enforcement operates in the case of serious felonies like kidnap or murder. Such incidents are thankfully rare and the majority of people will go through life never experiencing this sort of crime within their own circles. This means we glean any information about police procedure through consumption of media—news and TV shows in particular. However, there are marked differences between how law enforcement works in the media, and how it works in real life.

When we watch crime dramas on TV, especially when it comes to crimes against children, we see no expense is spared to save the child and bring the perpetrators to justice. Entire squads seem to be assigned to a single case, with characters at the top of the organizational hierarchy taking a keen personal interest, ordering junior police and detectives to drop everything to concentrate on that one crime.

Of course, TV shows are dramatized to entertain the audience. The exaggerated portrayal of the use of forensic science in criminal cases even has a term—the "CSI Effect"—named after long-running TV series *CSI: Crime Scene Investigation*, where every tiny scrap of evidence is analysed in laboratory conditions, discussed among senior scientists before being shared with the detectives assigned to the case. TV shows like CSI have given people unrealistic expectations about what technology can do, how extensive it can be, and how decisive the outcomes really are. Results of DNA or other evidence tests are often revealed on the spot on TV, whereas in reality, testing can take weeks, or even months to process. Furthermore, quite often the tests are imperfect and won't result in a match if they are too small a sample or have become contaminated.

What's more, many crime dramas, particularly the *Law & Order* franchise, are "ripped from the headlines"— that is, they are based on true crimes that have captured the public's interest. This can provide viewers with a skewed perception of how criminal investigations are handled in real life by police and other legal professionals. Often the stars are shown to go above and beyond, to take each case personally and work well outside of their official office hours as a matter of course. The team bounces ideas off each other, spotting clues and patterns in the most cryptic of circumstances and solves a double homicide in 40 minutes, all without ever having to file any paperwork.

Nevertheless, even if we are aware that our perceptions of how investigations are carried out may be colored by popular culture, we certainly expect a base level of honesty and competence when investigating a crime, particularly a crime against a child. Sadly, as can be seen in this book, this is not always the case, especially when the victim comes from a lower socioeconomic background or mixes in the "wrong" circles.

When it comes to the cases detailed in this book, only in the matter of Sian Kingi did law enforcement act in the manner in which we would expect in such a heinous case. In that case, the actions of the police are to be commended, and almost certainly prevented further tragedies from occurring.

In each of the other three tales presented here, the response of law enforcement was severely lacking in one way or another. Overworked and underfunded police departments in low income/high crime areas might be one explanation. The socio-economic status of the victim seems to come into play when resources are allocated to a case. And in some instances, outright corruption has dogged the investigation.

Taken too soon, these girls deserve to have their names remembered.

Shauna Howe, taken age 11
Sian Kingi, taken age 12
Leigh Leigh, taken age 14
Martha Puebla, taken age 16

PART I

SHAUNA HOWE (AGE 11)

PROLOGUE

I n August 2008, Oil City Council had an unusual attendee at the monthly meeting. Ten-year-old Elizabeth Roess waited patiently for her turn to speak, nervously clutching the piece of paper that held 175 signatures while going over in her mind the words she had been practicing for weeks.

Oil City, northwestern Pennsylvania, sits on a bend of the Allegheny River at the mouth of Oil Creek, about an hour and a half north of Pittsburgh. As its name suggests, the city was founded on the nearby oil fields and the wealth that came with the oil boom in the mid-to-late 1800s, and later when Pennsylvania held the mantle of "steelmaking capital of the world." At one time, the town boasted a population of 22,000, and was a great and prosperous place to live. Anybody who wanted to work could work. But later Oil City became the poster child for the rust belt, hit hard by the collapse of the U.S. steel industry in the 1980s.

Locals calculated the decline in Oil City's population by reference to each closing gas station. It became a town that offered a cheap cost of living, but gainful employment was scarce. As factories moved to the suburbs and entire industries were shifted offshore, jobs and people followed. The town had little to offer young people, many of whom dropped out of school long before their education was finished. It was one of those towns where most of the young were trapped in a cycle of poverty, and those who grew up and moved away never came back.

By 2008, Oil City was a struggling working-class town with a population of 10,500 and still going down. In many ways, it was typical of thousands of other rust-belt towns in America. Locals worked hard with what they had, parents tried to provide a better life for their children and the residents looked forward to local fairs and festivals to break the boredom, but the future was bleak for a large proportion of the population. Buildings of significance from better days were protected and restored so that at least parts of the town were picturesque. The hope was that visitors would stop and spend some money in the town, rather than barrel through on their way to somewhere more appealing.

However, there was one way in which Oil City was not like other towns at all. An entire generation had grown up there never truly experiencing one of America's most beloved festivals—Halloween. People were free to decorate their house inside and out and greet each other with a "Happy Halloween." The town tried to make things fun with the annual Pumpkin Bumpkin Festival, with music, food, spooky displays and face painting. But trick-or-treating, the cornerstone of the holiday, was banned from the minute the sun went down. Sending children door to door in the hopes of amassing a collection of candy was permitted only in daytime, when few people were home to dish out the goodies and the glow of jack-o'-lanterns was dulled by daylight. If kids wanted to dress up and go door to door at nighttime, they had to travel to a neighboring town, relying on parents to be willing and available to drive them, and visiting houses of total strangers.

That's why Elizabeth Roess was at the council meeting. The plucky ten-year-old was going to ask the council to let the kids have Halloween back. She had gathered signatures from everyone at school, other children who had grown up with TV shows and movies depicting the annual spooky event, but never experiencing a Halloween celebration of their own. This year, they wanted to go trick-or-treating on the night of October 31, right there in Oil City, their own town.

This was not a new debate for council. Whether or not to reinstate nighttime hours for the holiday had been debated in chambers for more years than most of the councilors could remember, but every year, daylight invariably won over the darkness. Unlike the children, those who sat on council remembered why Halloween had been outlawed in Oil City Pennsylvania sixteen years earlier, when pretend monsters had been displaced by real ones. Two crimes of unimaginable horror were seared in the minds of those who had lived their lives there, including all of the people listening to Elizabeth's petition. Little Elizabeth hadn't even been born, but she had been brought up knowing the story of the heinous acts that had come to define Oil City.

Nevertheless, she was there to tell the city that it was

time to move on. It was time to let the kids have the
Halloween that was so viciously stolen from them all that
time ago. But for some, the brutality of one night in
particular was etched in their memories. For some,
daylight would always win over darkness.

A HALLOWEEN PARTY

16 years earlier

It was October 27, 1992 and Oil City in Venango County, Pennsylvania, like every other town in America, was preparing for Halloween. Parents were raiding the shops for cheap bulk candy they could hand out to the miniature goblins, superheroes, witches and princesses that would be knocking on doors in a few days. As always, there were some households that went all-out with the decorations, adorning front porches and yards with life-sized witches riding broom or stirring cauldrons and jack-o'-lanterns lining the path to the front door. Others were happy with a single home-carved pumpkin and a candle recycled from the previous year.

Around the state, charities competed to put on the best haunted house, a favorite activity for the time of year. The blue-collar town of Oil City could never provide anything particularly fancy, but enough of the 12,000 residents got into the spirit of Halloween that the children looked forward to the spooky celebration each year.

Eleven-year-old Shauna Howe loved Halloween. She loved the decorations on the houses of her neighbors and friends, or hanging in the windows of the shops she passed on her way home from school. She loved spooky stories and the sugar rush of Halloween candy and the parties and celebrations that started a full week before the holiday culminated in the most exciting event of all: trick-or-treating on the night of the 31st.

The morning of the 27th she chattered to her mother, Lucy Howe, as she pulled on her clothes for the day. She would be going straight from school to join her Girl Scout troop to sing to residents at the local nursing home before heading to the First Free Methodist Church for a Halloween party. Shauna sang in the children's choir at the church, so she was looking forward to performing for the senior citizens, but she was looking forward to the party more. The family didn't have money to spend on any fancy dress costume, so Shauna improvised. She decided she would dress as a gymnast, wearing a turquoise gymnast's bodysuit with black stripes, tights, sneakers and soft satiny gloves that stretched up above her elbows. She wore the leotard underneath her regular clothes, as she would not have time to come home and change.

The 400 block of West First Street where Shauna lived with her mother and stepfather, Jon Brown, her twelve-year-old brother and five-year-old sister was in one of the poorer areas of the town. Nevertheless, it was not known to be particularly dangerous for children and there was the sense of security common in a small town whose residents rarely worried about locking houses and cars. Shauna's mother had no concerns about letting her daughter make her own way to and from school. She would, however, arrange to have Shauna picked up after her Halloween party, because Shauna was afraid to walk home in the dark. Lucy kissed Shauna goodbye and waved her on her way.

LATER THAT NIGHT, Lucy was at work in a pizza shop in Franklin, eight miles away, and called home to check on her family. Her de facto partner, Jon, told her that Shauna was not yet home. Lucy had forgotten that she was supposed to arrange to have Shauna picked up from the Girl Scout meeting, as the mother of the friend who usually brought Shauna home from Girl Scout activities was away. But the church was only half a mile away, along streets Shauna had traipsed many times before. Shauna knew her way home and would no doubt start walking when there was no familiar face to pick her up.

By 8.30 p.m., Shauna was still not home, long after she ought to have been, even if she had dawdled. Without the phone numbers of any of Shauna's friends whom she may have gone home with, Jon jumped into his car and drove the route Shauna was most likely to have taken home. There were a couple of paths the little girl could have taken, but she would certainly have stuck to the major roads. Arriving at the First Free Methodist Church, Jon confirmed that the Girl Scout party had long finished, and the girls had all gone home. More frustrated than frightened, he continued to drive around the nearby streets. Shauna, the only one of Lucy's children he had bonded with so far, was generally pretty obedient, but she could be headstrong. It would be unusual for her to simply take off to a friend's house without letting someone know, but not beyond the realms of possibility.

After exhausting the streets around the route home, Jon returned to home in case he had missed seeing Shauna and to be there to answer the phone if she was trying to call. Shauna still wasn't there, a fact Jon relayed to Lucy when she rang again at 9.30.

Lucy thought she knew where Shauna was most likely to be. Lucy had an acrimonious relationship with her former husband, Robert Howe, and police had been called to intervene in their disputes on more than one occasion. Of their four children, three lived with Lucy and one, Shauna's nine-year-old sister, lived with their father in a neighboring town. She called Robert's home phone, but he swore black and blue that Shauna wasn't with him.

Not sure whether or not to believe him, Lucy finished her shift and rushed home. Once there, she called the parents of Shauna's best friend, Joyeal Sines, who was part of the same Girl Scout group. Joyeal confirmed that Shauna had been at the party, and when it finished the two girls set off together in the same direction. When they got to where they needed to part ways, Shauna had asked Joyeal to walk her home, because she was frightened to walk in the dark. Joyeal refused but told Shauna she could come home with her, and then her father would walk her home. Shauna told her, "No, that's all right" and continued on the short walk towards home.

That had been at around 8 p.m., two hours previously. Shauna had not been more than ten minutes from home. At a little after 10.00 p.m., Lucy Howe called the police to report her little girl missing.

SNATCHED

When Oil City police received a call late on 27 October to say an eleven-year-old girl was missing, they were already investigating a report they had taken earlier that night of a very odd occurrence. That evening, Oil City resident Dan Paden had been walking along Reed Street when he noticed a young girl walking along West First Street and a man walking in the same direction on the opposite sidewalk. The girl was approaching the intersection where Reed and West First crossed, in front of a medical center and across the road from the Presbyterian church, a majestic stone building just a couple of blocks away from the modest home of Lucy and Jon. Dan was struck by the fact a young girl was out wearing just shorts and a T-shirt on such a cool evening.

Dan saw the tall thin man cross the road to the same side as the little girl and he appeared to scoop her up and run around the corner. Seconds later, Dan heard a muffled scream. He ran towards the intersection of West

First and Reed streets, only to see a small, boxy car pull away too quickly for him to catch any of the license plate number.

Nobody had a mobile phone in 1992, so Dan immediately began banging on the doors of the closest houses until a woman answered. Dan gasped to her, "I've just seen a little girl kidnapped and I need to call the police."

He provided the best description he could to the police. The man was tall, thin and scruffy-looking. He wore an army jacket and ball cap and was smoking a cigarette. The girl appeared slight—she was definitely a child and not an adult—wearing a top and shorts. He thought it was a small, boxy, dark red sedan he had seen driving away, possibly an Oldsmobile, with what he was certain was Pennsylvania plates. "I never saw her forced into the car," he told police. "I heard her scream. But as far as seeing him actually put her in the car, I didn't see that." He told them that there had been another person out walking at the time—a woman whom he judged to be in her sixties or seventies, who was walking west on West First Street and who may have been in a position to see the entire abduction.

Police took the report seriously, but with no record of a missing child, they had no way of knowing whether Dan had been accurate in what he had seen, or whether it was simply a father picking up his errant child. Dan was sure that he had witnessed a kidnapping. The girl had not seemed to know the man had been following her, and there was that little scream he had heard before the car sped away.

The phone call from Lucy Howe confirmed the worst-case scenario: they were dealing with a snatched child.

The Oil City police set up a roadblock on the roads out of town, and every police station within a ninety-nine-mile radius was informed. Local police combed the area by patrol car and on foot. They searched the home of Shauna's father, Robert Howe. Seeing this unusually flurry of police activity around the quiet streets, locals soon joined the search for the little girl.

By the next morning, word had spread throughout the entire town. There was barely a local soul who was unaware that eleven-year-old Shauna Howe was missing. Oil City did what small towns do best—they came together with a single goal, to get Shauna home safely. Groups of locals started gathering and conducting their own searches. By late morning, hundreds of volunteers were walking the streets and nearby forests looking for any signs of Shauna.

Lucy Howe couldn't leave the house in case Shauna had been kidnapped for ransom and the kidnappers called. It was a possible scenario, but unlikely as the family had no money to speak of. Helplessly, she paced back and forth like a caged animal, waiting for police or family members to bring her any news.

State troopers continued searching and door knocking, asking everyone along the route Shauna had taken whether they had seen anything. Apart from Dan Paden, nobody had. Detectives were not convinced that Dan was a particularly reliable or believable witness, and questioned him several times, even going to his workplace to do so. He remained steadfast in his story. The day turned into evening and then night, with no sign of Shauna or any clues as to who her abductor might be.

A GRIM DISCOVERY

The next day, October 29, Shauna's uncle, Keith Sibble, and a search party made up of friends and volunteers, decided to move their search into the nearby wooded areas. Like most small towns in that part of Pennsylvania, Oil City was bordered by forests, and reserves, many of which were rarely traversed.

They headed south and searched along Big Egypt Road in the Cranberry township, and went on to Waltonian Park, sixty acres of woodland with a few picnic areas. Then they went out to Coulter's Hole, a secluded swimming and camping spot in nearby Rockland Township, around seven-and-a-half miles south of Oil City, which would be picturesque if it weren't for the graffiti and trash. The hunting and fishing spot was popular with many people, including families, during the daytime, but became a no-go area for children after dark. By night it was frequented by wayward teens participating in underage drinking and drug taking, and troublemakers who met there to get smashed and fight. The Oil City chapter of a biker club, the Kingsmen, sometimes used it as a party spot. Police were often called out to investigate assaults and an array of illicit activities once the sun went down.

The group split up when they got to Coulter's Hole, but it was mere minutes later that one of the other men hollered for Keith Sibble. Leaning over the railing of a bridge that was part of a long-deserted railway, the searcher had spotted a flash of color that looked like a piece of child's clothing. When Keith peered over the rail, he felt sick. What lay below matched the description Lucy had given him of the bodysuit that Shauna had been wearing that day.

The search crew got word to the police. The police brought Shauna's stepfather, Jon Brown, to the scene, as he was familiar with the outfit she had worn to the Girl Scout party. Jon confirmed that the greenish slip of clothing was, indeed, the bodysuit Shauna had been wearing as part of her gymnast costume. Noting that there were some suspicious white marks on the material, police bagged the leotard and swarmed the area, looking for more clues. There were none to be found. It fell to Keith Sibble to tell his sister what the search party had discovered.

The discovery of the bodysuit was ominous and almost certainly pointed to sexual assault. Oil City didn't have the facilities to test the fabric, so it would have to be sent away. Police still hoped to find Shauna alive. The townsfolk continued their intensive search, now concentrating on the area where the slip of cloth had been found, with Shauna's uncles, Keith and Clair Sibble, among the volunteers.

The next day, October 30, dawned with gray, hazy, miserable weather conditions. The weather matched the mood of the searchers, many of whom were rapidly losing confidence that they would find the little girl alive. That day, their worst fears were realized. Just 500 yards from where her bodysuit was found, a man who had been camping in the area spotted a body below an abandoned railroad trestle in an almost dry, rocky creek bed. It was in a desolate, little-used area, difficult to see from the bridge above. Keith Sibble leaned far over the side of the bridge and saw his niece's body lying beneath the structure. He noticed she was wearing socks, but no shoes.

When police attended the scene, they were directed to a little girl lying face down, pinned between a rock and a log. There was little doubt that they had found Shauna Howe. She was wearing a short-sleeved shirt that was inside out and back to front, with the tag exposed near her throat. She also had on a pair of shorts and a pair of knee-high socks. Her feet were partially submerged in a shallow stream.

Shauna's uncles, Keith and Clair, were asked to identify the body. Both men confirmed that it was their niece, and fell into each other's arms, sobbing. The search for Shauna Howe had come to a devastating end.

Police immediately cordoned off the area and searched it carefully. Shauna's sneakers were spotted between the railroad ties in the framework of the trestle above where she had fallen. Either she had been running, tripped and fallen, or her abductor had thrown her down the thirty-three-foot drop and placed her shoes there to make it look like she'd tripped. They found a Blow Pop wrapper nearby, as well as an abandoned campsite. Police were confounded. They had searched the entire area the day before and they were positive if she had been there, they would have found her. They suspected that the killer had dumped her body in the past twenty-four hours, and may even have been part of the search party.

This time it fell to Clair to give his sister the news. He clomped up the stairs of the white double-story home, dreading the job he had to do. When Lucy opened the door, hoping for the best but fearful of the worst, he fell into her lap. All he could say was, "It's Shauna." Lucy let out the desperate wail of a mother who has lost her child.

Later, police made the formal notification to Shauna's mother and stepfather. Lucy confirmed that the shirt and shorts Shauna was wearing were hers, but she didn't know who the socks belonged to.

The knowledge that this was now a homicide kicked the investigation into the next gear. The townsfolk, most of whom were already aware of the missing little girl, feared abducted, were advised of the outcome. Oil City announced that Halloween was officially cancelled for the year and police urged all parents to keep a watchful eye on their kids and not let them out alone after dark. Parents needed no urging. There was a real bogeyman out there this year, and they weren't taking the risk of their children meeting him.

HALLOWEEN POSTPONED

On the evening of October 31, 1992, instead of trick-or-treating, hundreds of townsfolk took part in a silent candlelit procession to honor Shauna's memory. They prayed and comforted one another as they traced the steps of Shauna's final walk from the First Free Methodist Church, where she had been at her Girl Scout party, to the corner of Reed and West First streets, less than two blocks from the safety of her home.

The lab reports started coming into the investigating team. Shauna had been raped. She died from severe blunt force trauma that caused lethal head and chest injuries when she fell thirty-three feet from the railroad trestle to the ground below. Her knees had scuffs and scrapes on them, possibly from a rough floor where she was being held captive. The most horrifying detail was that when she fell or was thrown off the trestle, she was still alive. Shauna's body had slammed against an abutment and plummeted into the creek below, where she

lived for between five and thirty minutes before
succumbing to her injuries.

Shauna's bodysuit came back from the lab with
confirmation that the marks were seminal fluid. It was
still early days for DNA testing, but there were enough
bodily fluids found on Shauna's clothing to be useful.
The lab also kept swabs taken from Shauna's body in case
they could help identify her killer. A hair found on her
bodysuit did not match the DNA profile of the semen.

Abductions by strangers are exceedingly rare. In the
vast majority of homicides, the victim knows the perpetrator, or it is someone in the peripheral social circle of
their parents. Oil City was not immune to violent crime.
In the previous fifteen months, two women and a baby
boy had been killed. In each case, family members were
quickly arrested and the public had not been in any
danger. Detectives assumed that Shauna's case would be
no different. They had DNA. They just needed to find a
match, and the best place to start was at her home. There
was no central database of known criminals to test
against in those days, so the procedure was to test
everyone Shauna may have been in contact with in an
effort to both find the perpetrator and rule people out so
that investigations could be focused elsewhere.

Shauna's family was known to police and investigators
were immediately suspicious of the male members of the
family. Statistically, the most dangerous person in a
young girl's life is her mother's new partner. Shauna's
stepfather, Jon Brown, was the first to be tested and he
willingly provided his DNA. They also took samples from
her uncles, Keith and Clair Sibble. They grilled Keith in
particular, finding it somewhat coincidental that he had

been part of the search party that first decided to try Coulter's Hole, that led to the discovery of Shauna's bodysuit.

Shauna's mother accepted this extra intrusion on her family, but she drew the line when police wanted to DNA test her twelve-year-old son, Kerry John. Police insisted that it was merely to rule him out, but Lucy was horrified. Eventually, Kerry John himself insisted she let him provide a sample, willing to do anything to help find the person who hurt his sister.

Neither the DNA tests nor the questioning of Shauna's various family members yielded any sort of positive result for the investigation. Although they didn't rule anyone out, with no hits on the family, investigators started to look into every adult male that Shauna and her family knew. They questioned neighbors, teachers and family friends, as well as the fathers of all the girls Shauna knew from school and Girl Scouts. They grilled every male who worked at Shauna's school, and those in the shops she visited.

Men who fit the description provided by Dan Paden were given priority, such as tall lanky Ted Walker, who worked at the pizza shop and who always wanted a hug from the young girls who came in. Shauna and her friends went out of the way to avoid him and spoke to each other about how creepy he was. He was a smoker (Dan had seen the man smoking) and had been known to drive a small red car, although his current car was a Chevrolet Monte Carlo, and not red. Ted Walker told police he knew nothing and submitted to a DNA test. There was no match to either the semen or the hair.

Another man with an unsavory past who lived just

doors away from where Shauna was abducted was Michael Kucewicz. He left town on a bus the day after her body was found and had yet to return. He became a prime suspect, but detectives had no way of knowing where he had gone.

Detectives were also suspicious of the man who found Shauna's body in a little-used area after police had apparently failed to. What was he doing out there? Although not a perfect match for the description they had, he drove a small red car. Then there was Dan Paden, whose police still weren't sure they believed. How was it he didn't see the man put Shauna into the car and then climb into the car himself when it would have taken just seconds to get to the corner after the girl screamed? Why hadn't he tried to help Shauna the moment she was grabbed? Why hadn't the other potential witness Dan said he had seen that night not come forward, despite police pleas?

Both the searcher and Dan submitted to DNA tests. Neither was a match.

On Monday, November 2nd, 150 people attended the funeral of Shauna Howe. An already-tragic event was made worse by the knowledge that police already had hundreds of suspects on their radar, but no solid leads or evidence. The mourners couldn't help but look around and wonder: was the murderer among them?

Shauna was laid to rest while her favorite song, Billy Ray Cyrus's *Achy Breaky Heart*, played over the loudspeakers.

A TOWN GRIPPED BY FEAR

Two weeks later, the residents of Oil City had not received any official updates about the investigation into Shauna Howe's death. If detectives had any news, they weren't sharing it, leaving people with nothing but rumors, speculation and fearmongering. Most people believed the abductor and murderer to be a local, probably someone who knew Shauna. Shauna's family were treated with suspicion, with many people finding it a little too convenient that her own uncles had been part of the search party that found her clothes. Children were traumatized, crawling into bed with their parents, unable to sleep in case the Bad Man came for them at night. One sick vandal spray-painted a wall near Shauna's school warning elementary school students that they could be next.

Oil City became a town gripped by fear. Children were no longer allowed to roam the streets and their parents waited with them at the bus stop until they were safely on board on their way to school. Some of the local kids needed counselling. Police rummaged through Shauna's desk and asked her classmates questions about her and whether she had ever visited their houses. One friend from Girl Scouts recounted that Shauna had two Blow Pops and the little girl asked if she could have one. Shauna had refused the request, claiming she was saving one lollipop for herself and the other for her mother. The blow pop wrapper found near Coulter's Hole went up the list of significant evidence.

The mothers of three of Shauna's schoolmates started a child-safety group called Operation Kid Watch. At its first meeting, about 100 people gathered in a church to trade suggestions about guarding their children and demand answers from the police. Venango County Sheriff, Gene Price, advised the crowd that hundreds of people had provided information that investigators were sifting through and urged the parents to be patient. In the meantime, he suggested girls should travel in groups of three or more, parents should know when to expect their children home and should tell their children to telephone once they reached their destinations.

Some parents admitted giving their girls mace to carry in their bags. Another suggested arming girls with cans of hairspray as a low-tech substitute. The sheriff strongly warned against this plan, as an attacker could easily turn such items against the children. The meeting did little to assuage the fears of the people who wanted answers, not weaponry, for their kids.

On 16 November, the Oil City Rotary Club put up a $500 reward for any information that led to the arrest of Shauna's murderer and police issued a request for information about an early 1980s dull-red Oldsmobile Omega.

Posters of a similar car were tacked up across town, taped to shop doors and stapled to utility poles. Police got hundreds of calls and investigated hundreds of cars. They sifted through them all, but none of the cars seemed to belong to the abductor.

An eerie quiet descended on Oil City as the residents stayed indoors after dark and waited for news that the monster had been captured. News that never came.

A COLD CASE

Two years passed, with police apparently no closer to making an arrest. The Oil City Council had put up a $5000 reward for information, and Venango County Crime Stoppers added another $1000. A month later, an anonymous donor added another $5000. With the $500 already offered by the Rotary Club, this brought the total reward offered to $11,500, a substantial sum for most Oil City residents. But if anybody knew anything, they were keeping quiet.

Oil City had lost its safe, small-town feel. Streets remained empty at night and the doors of the Seventh Street Elementary were always locked when not in use. Citizens quietly seethed at police, blaming them not just for failing to arrest someone, but also for refusing to share details of the investigation.

The council voted to ban trick-or-treating after dark until the murderer was found. No parent would have allowed their child out at night anyway. The fear had spread to neighboring towns, where miniature goblins and witches now only knocked on doors of people they knew while holding tightly to the hands of their mothers.

Little seemed to have been done, as far as the residents were concerned. Whenever a similar crime occurred in the vicinity, or even in neighboring states, the newspapers announced that police were "investigating links." None of those investigations ever seemed to go anywhere.

The FBI released a profile of the killer, in the hope that some detail might resonate with someone about the behavior or actions of a person they knew at the time. It suggested he was a white male of average size, possibly in his twenties, who held a menial job and had his own form of transportation. They said that he was likely to have suddenly taken time off work or consumed more alcohol and drugs immediately after Shauna's murder. He had probably been overly interested in news reports about her death. Citizens were told to try and recall anyone who may have been fired, skipped social gatherings, altered his meals or sleep, fought with friends, taken a sudden vacation or appeared to be nervous or preoccupied around the time of Shauna's murder. The profiler said it was unlikely the killer had struck before, but he could not rule out the possibility that the person would strike again.

The profile could have applied to half the displaced men in the county. It did little to help with the investigation.

In July 1995, police received a report of a violent attempted abduction of a young woman on east Second Street, not far from where Shauna was taken. The twenty-two-year-old had been followed out of a bar by a man she had met there. He had grabbed her, tried to force her into the trunk of his car and slammed her head against the sidewalk cement when she resisted. When he realized that he wouldn't be able to immediately get the injured woman into the trunk, the man sped away.

Upon hearing the victim's description of her attacker, police knew exactly where to look. They were sure it was one of the O'Brien brothers.

Tim and Jim O'Brien were well-known to police. They had lived in Oil City all of their lives, working factory and gardening jobs when they weren't in prison. People who worked with the brothers, especially women, described being in a permanent state of anxiety around them, never sure when an uncomfortable encounter or a violent explosion was coming. They were first arrested as young teens and ran afoul of the law continuously there-after. Between the two of them, the brothers, both in their twenties, had clocked up a string of offences, including sexual offences against both adults and children.

The older of the two, Tim O'Brien, was in prison at the time of the young woman's attempted abduction, having pleaded guilty to corruption of minors after getting a sixteen-year-old drunk and taking pornographic pictures of her earlier that year. Jim O'Brien, however, was identified as the assailant. He was arrested and convicted of first-degree felony attempted kidnapping, simple assault and unlawful restraint. He was given a lengthy jail sentence of ten to twenty years, the judge noting that Jim O'Brien was a menace to society, having already been arrested twice in 1989, once in 1990, and again in 1992, 1993 and 1994.

Naturally everyone wondered if the O'Brien brothers

had been suspects in Shauna's rape and murder. In fact, they would have been prime suspects but for two things: nobody could mistake either of the dumpy O'Briens for a tall, slender man and, more importantly, they had both been in prison at the time of Shauna's murder. As far as alibis went, it was a strong one. Their names had been crossed off the list of potential suspects long ago.

It was nearly three years after the slaying, and it was just another promising lead that went nowhere.

As TIME WORE ON, the trail appeared to have gone cold. Locals were reminded of the little girl who had gone missing thanks to a small wreath on a telephone pole bearing Shauna's photograph that marked the street corner where she was abducted. Around town, posters featuring Raphael, one of the Teenage Mutant Ninja Turtles, encouraging children to "say no," "get away" and "call a safe number" were beginning to curl and fade. Nevertheless, the mystery of who killed Shauna was still in the forefront of many citizens' minds, especially those who had children.

Every year on October 27, the residents held their candlelight vigil and marched the last path Shauna had taken on her fateful walk home that night. Oil City didn't celebrate Halloween. Instead, police provided an update, stating that they continued to search for Shauna's killer. They still believed her murderer was a local and reminded the public of the details in the FBI profile. In a statement to the press, they said they had followed up leads in California, Ohio, New York and Kansas, but the trail kept leading back to Oil City. The killer most likely walked among them.

Then the worst fears of Oil City resurfaced. On October 29, 1997, almost five years to the day after Shauna Howe was snatched, another little girl went missing.

THE BOGEYMAN'S RETURN?

Four-year-old Shenee Freeman had been playing with her friends Christian and Tiffany in a grassy area near Fern Court, a council housing estate in Oil City. Christian had cut himself and run inside to see his mother. While he was gone, Tiffany reported that she had seen a man in black take Shenee into the woods. Oil City's worst nightmare had come true. The bogeyman was back for Halloween.

Word spread like wildfire. All the people in town were hyper-aware of the earlier abduction. There were always news reports and features around Halloween time, and the annual memorial walk had taken place the night before last. Had the murderer struck again, five years later? Was Halloween a special time for him?

A hundred volunteers leapt into action, joining police and firefighters in the search for Shenee. The memory of the tragic outcome of a similar search five years earlier was like a nightmare revisited. A description was circulated: Shenee was wearing a long-sleeved white cotton dress with a large red heart on the front and four hearts on the skirt. She wore bright blue socks and white sneakers and had her hair in pigtails, one tied with a red ribbon, the other purple. As temperatures dropped, people became more worried, because she was not wearing a coat. Searchers hoped she had found somewhere sheltered like a dog kennel or barn, as her light dress would not be enough protection in the night.

As day turned into night, police became suspicious of someone in the search party. Nicholas Bowen was known to the parents of Shenee's friends and had been playing with the children earlier. He was wearing black. He had earlier hugged Shenee's mother and told her not to worry, but as the search went on, he became agitated and wanted to go home.

It didn't take much questioning by the police to make Nicholas break down. He led them to a shallow grave in the woods very close to where the children had been playing. Twelve hours after she had gone missing, police recovered the body of Shenee Freeman and charged Nicholas Bowen with her murder. He had sexually assaulted her, and then thrown her into a ravine, where she hit her head and bled profusely. Panicking, Nicholas had kicked dirt, sticks and leaves over her before running back to the house, not sure whether she was dead or alive.

Naturally, Nicholas was an attractive suspect in the prior abduction of Shauna Howe, but there was one problem. He was a seventeen-year-old schoolboy. The tall, bushy-haired teen would have been barely twelve when Shauna was murdered. Any possible connection was ruled out. He would have been too young to have carried out her murder—the date of the two murders was merely a shocking, terrifying coincidence.

Oil City had another reason not to celebrate Halloween.

NO SHORTAGE OF SUSPECTS

Later that year, Richard Jobes from Armstrong County, a little over an hour south of Oil City, was convicted on fifteen counts of indecent assault. The victims were the three nurses who had been hired to look after his sick children, a two-year-old child with cerebral palsy and an infant with a breathing disorder. Richard had originally faced over 200 charges, but most were dropped in return for a plea. His wife, Diane Jobes, was convicted of simple assault, terroristic threats and harassment. One nurse said that Diane held her down while Richard tried to rape her. In sentencing, the judge said, "The depravity that went on is hard to comprehend even as a judge."

Shortly after Richard's sentencing, Diane told police that she had lied about her husband's alibi the night of Shauna's death. The couple had lived about eight miles from Shauna's house at the time of her murder.

Police relaunched the Shauna Howe case and thoroughly questioned Richard Jobes about Shauna and his whereabouts that night. However, his DNA was not a match and there was no other evidence linking him to the crime. Jobes became just one of more than 2000 men who had been questioned over the past five years. It was another dead end. Diane Jobes had likely been hoping to get a reduction in her own sentence by throwing extra shade on her husband.

Once again, Shauna Howe was relegated to the cold case files.

Around this time, Lucy Howe got a computer and learned how to look up sex offenders in the area. Megan's Law, named after a New Jersey girl who had been murdered by a repeat sexual offender, required certain sex offenders to register their whereabouts with police following their release from prison. In cases of dangerous predators, the law also allowed for limited community notification.

Lucy was shocked to see how many sexual deviants were living within blocks of her house, where had Shauna lived. There were twenty registered in Oil City alone. Lucy could no longer bear to live in a town where she had to wonder about every man she came into contact with. She sold her house, packed up her remaining family and moved to North Carolina.

NEARLY TWO YEARS LATER, on October 27, 1999, police made their annual statement to the press. This time they claimed they had obtained evidence recently that they "felt would be beneficial in presenting a prosecutable case." The FBI was analyzing the new evidence and, they said, "We are feeling very good about the case as it stands today."

A couple of months earlier, police had searched a yellow brick home on Reed Street, near where the abduction took place. At the time Shauna went missing, Michael Kucewicz, who had jumped on a bus and disappeared the day after Shauna's body was found, was renting it. He had been a person of interest ever since and was currently serving time in a Connecticut prison on drugs-related charges. Kucewicz, who vaguely fit the description provided by Dan Paten, had been questioned many times since police tracked him down. He had submitted to blood tests and polygraph tests, but he remained an attractive suspect for police, despite the absence of concrete evidence.

Police didn't say what caused them to search the house that day, but their search concentrated on the basement and a space under the back porch stairs where media surmised the scuffs on Shauna's knees may have come from.

In a most unusual move, Michael Kucewicz wrote a letter from prison to *The Derrick*, Oil City's local newspaper. He wrote, "Well, God rest her soul, and with all due respect for the Howe family, her death has been a misery to me. Misery to the point of seven year's worth of questions, blood tests, polygraph tests and more done to me because, I'm told, being a male with a minor criminal record, I am a major suspect."

Once again, these enquiries apparently went nowhere, and police provided no more updates to the press. Children were kept inside on Halloween night for the seventh year running.

A HAPHAZARD INVESTIGATION

Detective Richard Graham was becoming frustrated. He had joined the Pennsylvania State Police in 1970 and was a patrolman when Shauna Howe went missing. Although he had been part of the search crew at the time, he'd had little involvement for several years afterwards. The lead investigator on Shauna's case retired in 1995, and for a while nobody had taken over. Six months later, in 1996, it was assigned to Richard Graham as a cold case. He visited Lucy personally and promised her that he would find Shauna's killer, no matter how long it took.

One of the sad lessons that Richard had learned over his years in the police force was that law enforcement agencies had limited resources, which meant they had to prioritize their cases according to a variety of factors. Cold cases, or cases where little new information was coming in, were often given the lowest priority.

Television is a terrible culprit in giving a very skewed impression to people about the amount of resources dedicated to cases. If Shauna Howe had a TV drama team working her case, no doubt it would have been solved long ago. TV crime dramas often depict large teams of experts working together, dedicated to solving one partic-ular case, with exotic laboratories of high-tech equipment at their disposal.

The truth, especially in struggling working-class towns, is invariably much more disappointing. Investiga-tions can often be haphazard, people come and go, some-times taking knowledge with them. People fail to follow up leads or forget to make case notes or share informa-tion with others on the team. Absconding suspects may not be aggressively pursued. Crime scenes may not be thoroughly searched, resulting in lost evidence. Some cases are simply closed due to the inability to devote the necessary time and resources to resolve them. Law enforcement officers are often overworked, handling many cases at once. There had been so many calls in the Shauna Howe case that the police had been unable to keep up and there was no precise tally anywhere. There was a good chance that some information from those calls had never been recorded and was lost forever. In fact, when gathering information for this book, it has been difficult to align the timelines of certain events, with different information coming from news stories, court records and recollections of police and witnesses in interviews.

Richard Graham was one of those overworked police officers, with a workload of up to seventy open files at a time. But the murder of the little girl haunted him, and he spent his own time revisiting Shauna Howe's case, at home, outside of work hours. He contacted the lab technician who worked on the case and asked how confident he was about the DNA. Some detectives had surmised that it was possible the DNA could have been transferred to Shauna's bodysuit independently of her murder, particularly as the house she lived in was not well-kept and many people came and went. However, later, when DNA testing became more precise, Richard ordered a test on a swab that had been taken from Shauna's mouth. That swab tested positive for the same seminal DNA that was on her clothing. The technician told Rich, "If you find the DNA match, you'll have the killer."

From that moment on, Rich collected and tested DNA from as many people as he could, sometimes even from deceased men in the area. Bit by bit, he built up a database of men who had contact with Shauna.

As the years went on and leads went stale, Richard thought that fresh eyes on the evidence could be beneficial. He sought the services of noted criminal profiler Colonel Robert Ressler. Robert had helped catch the Son of Sam killer, David Berkowitz, and his techniques helped inspire the movie "Silence of the Lambs." Robert made a suggestion that had not really been canvassed by the police on Shauna's case: what if Shauna was abducted and murdered not by one person, but by two, or even more, people? That could explain why the witness, Dan Paden, hadn't seen the abductor put Shauna in the car and then hop into the driver's seat himself, even though it had taken just seconds to run to the corner. That detail had been one of the reasons police had been suspicious of his version of events. If the abductor had handed her to someone else and run away, the witness's account made more sense.

Around late October or early November 2001, Richard's investigation of another old case, a violent robbery that had taken place at the Oil City Moose Club, brought him to the Venango County Jail to question a suspect who was serving time for another crime. The suspect was well-known to police in the area. It was the older of the O'Brien brothers, Tim. He was in prison on burglary charges, while his brother Jim was still serving his sentence for his attempt to shove a young woman in the trunk of his car in 1995.

Tim O'Brien didn't have much to say about the robbery, in which a security guard had been badly beaten, tied up and shoved into a refrigerator. As Richard left the room, he did what had become a habit for him with every male criminal local to Oil City—he asked if Tim would provide a DNA sample for the Shauna Howe case. Tim O'Brien was startled, but said, "OK, but I have to check with my lawyer first." Something about the way he said it made the hairs on the back of Richard's neck prickle. He awaited the return of the test with anticipation.

Tim O'Brien's sample came back negative for a match on the seminal fluid, but Richard couldn't shake the feeling that something was wrong. That feeling increased tenfold in early December 2001, during a meeting with state parole agent Ed Flick on an unrelated matter. The conversation turned to Shauna Howe and Ed commented that he had always felt the O'Briens could have been involved. It seemed like their modus operandi. However, their alibi was airtight. Alibis don't get much stronger than being in prison at the time the crime occurred.

Following that conversation, for the first time it

occurred to Richard that he had always relied on word of mouth about the O'Brien brothers' whereabouts at the time of Shauna's abduction. He had inherited the case with a note to the effect that they had been ruled out as suspects due to their incarceration, but had never checked official records himself. He made a note to double-check, just to satisfy the niggling doubt.

What he discovered rocked him to the core. Somewhere along the way there had been an error made, paperwork that was wrong or a miscommunication. The official records showed that the O'Briens had indeed been arrested around that time, but they had made bail and were not in custody when Shauna was abducted.

Tim and Jim O'Brien went straight to the head of the suspect list. Richard sought another DNA test, this time on the single hair that had been found on Shauna's bodysuit.

BLOOD BROTHERS

Richard Graham's next priority was to obtain a sample from Jim O'Brien for a DNA test. Unfortunately, before he could arrange to see Jim in the Mercer State correctional facility, on December 20, 2001, Richard was transferred to a new unit, which meant being removed from the case. His final act before transfer was to request that one of his fellow troopers visit Jim O'Brien and request a DNA sample. That DNA sample was taken from Jim O'Brien in early January 2002.

While they were awaiting the results of Jim O'Brien's DNA test, the case took another surprising turn. On January 9, 2002, Tim O'Brien's former cellmate at the Venango County Prison, Ryan Heath, told police that Tim had made a confession over a game of cards when the prisoners were in lockdown on September 11, 2001. Heath told police that Tim O'Brien confided that he threw Shauna in the trunk of a vehicle and then off a bridge.

When Richard had revisited Shauna's case, he noticed something he hadn't seen before in some of the photographs. There was a shoe print on Shauna's cheek, something nobody had made note of in the file. This had been a violent attack, but there were no signs of any restraints, no ligature marks around her wrists or ankles as may be expected. Somehow Shauna had been kept alive without being restrained, and whoever had raped her had reclothed her. To Richard, this lent weight to the theory that more than one person had been involved in Shauna's abduction and murder.

The O'Brien brothers were known to be close and to carry out crimes together. Jim O'Brien was generally considered to be the more dominant of the two, despite being younger, due to Tim's learning difficulties and myriad of mental health problems. The brothers were looking better for this crime all the time. If the DNA was a match, they could possibly close this case, nearly a decade later.

In early February 2002, Richard Graham took a call from the FBI lab technician who had worked on the Shauna Howe case for years. Despite Richard no longer being assigned to the case, she wanted him to be the first to know the news. Jim O'Brien's DNA was a match for that which was found on Shauna Howe's bodysuit and in her mouth. Tim O'Brien's DNA matched the hair found on her bodysuit.

Before relaying the information to Jim O'Brien, law enforcement officers, including state police, FBI agents and a couple of FBI headquarters detectives, met to strategize. The DNA match was strong evidence, but it was not conclusive on its own. The fact that it was a match for one person did not preclude it being a match for other people. Neither Tim nor Jim O'Brien matched the witness's description of the man that Dan Paden had seen snatch Shauna, nor did either of them have a small red sedan. Other than a story from an unreliable jailhouse snitch, there was no other evidence linking them to the crime. Any decent lawyer would tear the case to shreds, even with the DNA evidence.

Now that they had come to the conclusion that more than one person had probably carried out the crime, the investigators wondered if there could even be a third person involved? The idea that such a crime could be carried out by three people in the town bordered on the unthinkable, but they were willing to entertain the thought if it provided answers.

There was one man in town detectives kept coming back to. Ted Walker was a tall, thin, scruffy smoker. He knew Shauna and had a reputation of being inappropriate around young girls. And most importantly of all, he knew the O'Briens. In fact, one of the O'Brien brothers was staying at his residence around the time of the abduction because Ted needed help on some maintenance jobs. Ted's place was known to be a flophouse where anyone could stay and where there were few rules. Ted had owned a car matching the description provided by Dan Paden, although it wasn't an Oldsmobile. When he had been questioned in early days, an FBI agent had seen a red car behind his house. Ted had said it was an inoperable project he was working on, incapable of being driven. Nobody checked. The car had long ago been sent for scrap.

The investigative team believed they had good reason to bring in Ted Walker for questioning once more. This time they had some information for him: police told him they had a DNA hit and witness evidence on the O'Briens.

Ted had a habit of changing details of his statements every time he was questioned, although that happened with many of the witnesses detectives grilled over the years. Most of the men had something to hide, even if they had nothing to do with Shauna Howe. An analysis of Ted's previous written statements showed he had devoted much time and thought to completing the form and had given lengthy answers, unlike most men who gave short, direct responses.

He changed his story again this time, making some new admissions. He told investigators that he may have taken in some "real bad people" who may have done "a disgusting thing." He also admitted to knowing the O'Brien brothers and said that the three of them had been joking around about how stupid the Oil City cops were and that it would be funny to snatch a child in front of a witness on Halloween and watch as the cops made fools of themselves running around looking for the kid. Once they had caused a bit of chaos, they would return the kid safely. They would grab someone they knew so that the kid wouldn't be too scared.

Police listened to this astonishing story and asked for Ted's consent to search his house, which would avoid having to show probable cause to a judge to obtain a warrant. According to Richard Graham, later that night a neighbor called the fire department and reported that Ted was burning something behind his house, which Richard understood to be a mattress. That prompted the investigators to get a search warrant. Late in the evening of Thursday March 14, 2002, state police and the FBI converged on the home of Ted Walker at 43 Laurel Avenue in Oil City.

Laurel Avenue, a quiet, unsealed road, lay on the edge of town. It was lined with ramshackle, derelict houses with overgrown, neglected yards between them. It was not a street that parents would have been happy for their kids to visit, and it is doubtful it would have been included in the trick-or-treating route back when Halloween was still celebrated in Oil City. It was the kind of house you could carry a kidnapped child into, without worrying about the neighbors seeing, or even if they did, they would turn a blind eye, not wanting to become involved.

Ted, who worked casual night shifts, was not home at the time of the search and police would not make any official statement to reporters. Somehow though, word got out that the search was related to the Shauna Howe case. Local media ran with the news and printed Ted Walker's picture alongside the story.

When Dan Paden saw that picture, he picked up the phone and called the police. Dan Paden was 90% sure that Ted was the tall, thin, smoking man he had seen all those years ago near the corner of Reed and West First streets.

During Ted's next interview, even more revelations came out. This time, he admitted to approaching Shauna that night, asking her about Girl Scout cookies and giving her a hug, before snatching her around the shoulders and handing her over to Tim O'Brien as part of their prank. Following the abduction, he said he returned to his home and a few minutes later, Jim and Tim O'Brien came to his house and carried Shauna up the stairs. Walker claimed he hadn't said anything earlier because he feared for his son's life. The O'Brien brothers had threatened to kill the kid if he ever said anything.

Five days after that interview, on March 19, 2002, Jim O'Brien was told that his DNA was a match. When detectives set the report in front of him, Jim reportedly dropped his head almost to his lap and said, "All right. I'm not going to sit here and deny what you already know."

However, when reporters arrived to interview him, Jim remained defiant. He confirmed to the media that he had provided a state trooper with a DNA sample and that an FBI agent had told him he was a match. But he insisted he was not involved in the crime. He told local newspaper *The Derrick*, "I didn't do it, so I wasn't going to admit to it. I have a clear conscience. I don't know how you would go on living knowing you were responsible for a child's death like that. I understand why they want it solved. It's a horrific crime."

Despite all the information and evidence that police now had that pointed to three culprits—the O'Brien brothers and Ted Walker—the district attorney needed a watertight case. The county did not have much money and the district attorney knew that each suspect would be entitled to two state-appointed lawyers. They had to wait until they had a case that would most likely result in a conviction, as well as the budget available to prosecute.

One thing they couldn't account for was where Shauna had been held for the two days before she had been killed and her body found. There was no evidence found in Ted's house that she had been held there.

Richard Graham believed she had been held at a campsite near where her body was later found.

The O'Brien brothers were locked away safely while investigators built their case. Jim was still serving a sentence for attempted kidnapping. Tim had been on house arrest for assault charges, and in May 2003 he was sentenced and labelled a sexually violent predator, the most severe classification of sex offender, for indecently assaulting a six-year-old girl and an eleven-year-old boy in 1999 and 2000. At his Megan's Law hearing, Tim had been assessed to have both antisocial personality disorder and pedophiliac tendencies.

It was two more years before the district attorney was ready to move on the case. Finally, on July 3, 2004, Tim and Jim O'Brien were charged with first- and second-degree murder, rape, involuntary deviate sexual intercourse and kidnapping.

JUSTICE FOR SHAUNA

This was the biggest news story in Oil City for a long time. The affidavit for the arrest of the O'Briens included details about Ted Walker's role in the abduction. When news crews converged on his house to ask what he thought of the arrest, he expressed relief that police had finally caught the culprits, saying, "Good for them. I hope they cut their heads off. I thought they were friends of mine, they tried to say I was a part of this and destroyed my life."

Ted said that he had only been interviewed about the case in the past because he matched the description of the abductor. When pressed about details that were contained in the affidavit, he denied everything, saying, "I never met the little girl, I don't even know who her mother is." He asserted he wasn't at home on the evening of her abduction and that he had no respect for anyone that would hurt a child. He said police coerced him into saying he was at the scene by threatening to take his son away and that they had planted evidence when they searched his home, knowing he was at work.

The next day, Saturday July 4, state police officers sat outside the multi-story derelict house at 43 Laurel Avenue. They spent the morning documenting the comings and goings at the residence, before arresting Ted Walker without incident at about 11.45 a.m.

Under questioning, Ted quickly realized his lies had caught up with him. The next day he agreed to a plea deal. He would plead guilty to kidnapping and third-degree murder, which carried a prison term of twenty to forty years. In return for his testimony against the two brothers at their trial, he would not be charged with first- or second-degree murder, the former carrying a possible death penalty and the latter life in prison.

Trooper Vernon Brown interviewed Ted Walker, who gave him a detailed account of his version of the events of October 1992. According to Ted, the initial plan was to be seen grabbing a child on Halloween night, making it obvious enough that the police would be called, keep the child for ten to fifteen minutes, and then drop the child off at home. It was supposed to be a prank to upset the Oil City Police Department and make them look incompetent. The joke had been cooked up by the O'Brien brothers, who had just been released on bail. The plan was to grab ten-year-old Johnny Eckonen, a friend of Ted's son, as it would be a bonus to frighten Johnny and his mother.

Once this plan was formed in the O'Briens' minds, they discussed the abduction idea with increasing frequency and intensity. On the night of October 27, Ted said he had driven to the A-Plus convenience store for coffee and cigarettes when he saw the O'Briens drive by in one of Ted's fixer-upper cars, a red Chevrolet Chevette, which he said they took without his permission. Ted followed them to West First and Reed streets, where both cars pulled over.

Ted got out of his car and approached the brothers. Tim O'Brien told him, "We've bumped up the plan." They wanted to snatch a kid tonight, and they didn't care who it was. At that moment, the men saw Shauna walking down the dark street. Ted approached her, asking if she was selling Girl Scout cookies and if she would give him a hug. He scooped her up and shoved her toward Tim O'Brien, who was standing at the open passenger side door of the two-door Chevette. He had one foot propped on the floorboard and one on the street. The front seat had been pulled forward, ready to shove Shauna into the back seat. Jim was at the wheel.

Once the brothers had her in the car, Ted said he jumped in his own car, circled the block and saw that the red Chevette had gone. After stopping for more coffee and a loaf of bread, he went home

Shortly after he arrived home, the brothers arrived with Shauna under their arms. Tim held the upper portion of her body, holding her face into his torso to muffle her attempts to scream, and Jim held her legs. They carried her up to the second story while Ted started dinner for his son in the kitchen. He claimed he still believed it to be part of the joke they had discussed.

He was cooking spaghetti when he heard a female voice above crying, "Get off me, let me up, let me go." Ted said he stormed upstairs and called through the door, telling the brothers to get the hell out of his house. Tim

O'Brien came to the door told him to mind his own business and worry about his own son.

Ted said he left the residence for a short time. When he returned, the brothers and Shauna were no longer there. Walker was furious that the O'Brien brothers had brought Shauna to his home. When they returned without her, between the late evening hours of October 27 and the early morning hours of October 28, he kicked them out.

Detectives still didn't trust Ted one bit. They were sure he had spun his tale to paint himself as innocent and in a way that would be most beneficial to him when it came to sentencing. But he was their best bet for finally getting a conviction for the crime that had hung over Oil City for nearly thirteen years. They had to work with Ted. They needed his testimony.

For the first time since Shauna Howe was abducted, things moved quickly. The trial was moved out of Venango County because the high profile of the case, the decade of living in fear and mistrust, the reputation of the O'Brien brothers and the disgust and anger of the local residents meant it was unlikely the accused could get a fair trial locally. The court ruled that the O'Brien brothers be tried together and that Ted Walker would have a separate trial afterwards.

When the trial started, Lucy Howe, Jon Brown and Shauna's uncles, Keith and Clair Sibble, sat quietly in the courtroom, listening to every word.

Ted Walker testified but once again changed parts of his story, just as he had every time he had been interviewed. In his initial confession, he had told police that he had seen the O'Brien brothers carrying Shauna upstairs. Now his story was that, after stopping for more coffee and a loaf of bread, he went home and learned from his son that the O'Briens had taken someone upstairs. He didn't ask, but he guessed that someone was Shauna.

The O'Brien brothers' lawyers claimed that Ted Walker was the sole culprit of both the rape and murder and that he was lying in order to save himself. According to the defense, Ted wasn't just buying coffee on October 27, 1992, he was waiting for Shauna to leave her Girl Scout party. He had testified that he did not know Shauna, but the defense lawyers presented two witnesses, including Ted's niece and a former co-worker, who testified that he had met Shauna at the pizza shop and that his son had been known to play with her. Jim O'Brien's attorney, Wayne Hundertmark, told the jury, "Ted Walker is evil. He's every parent's, every neighbor's worst nightmare... He's a child molester and he's a liar. He's hoping he gets less time because he's a weasel and he turned other people in."

The most compelling evidence was Jim O'Brien's DNA on Shauna's bodysuit and in her mouth. Jim's attorney claimed that his semen was found on her body and in her mouth because Jim had had sex in that bed earlier in the day, with a woman named Heather, whom he had picked up in a bar. He said that when Ted took Shauna into the bed and molested her, Jim's semen was transferred to Shauna's bodysuit, which Ted then stuffed into her mouth to stop her from crying out.

However, Jim's attorney couldn't explain why his was the only male DNA on the bodysuit, and Shauna's was the only female DNA. There was no DNA from the mysterious Heather, whom Jim's team was unable to produce for trial and, most significantly, no DNA from Ted Walker.

James Goodwin, representing Tim O'Brien, claimed there was not a single piece of credible evidence to link Tim to the case. He was only on trial because of his brother's DNA and the history of the O'Brien brothers doing things together. The hair could have been transferred from Jim. Most of the evidence against Tim O'Brien came from a jailhouse snitch, Ryan Heath, who said that Tim had confessed to him over a card game on September 11, 2001, when the prison was in lockdown. However, Ryan Heath was not a trustworthy or reliable witness, and his credibility was thrown into doubt when it was established that he had fabricated some details of Tim O'Brien's alleged confession.

The jury made a field trip to Oil City, where they walked the route that Shauna walked on the night of her abduction. They were also taken to the abandoned railway bridge—by this time a popular cycling path—to see where Shauna's body was found.

Each day, the brothers waited for the jurors to leave before they were shackled and let out of the courtroom. The jurors were not allowed to know that the O'Briens were serving jail time on other charges while they were being tried for Shauna's murder, in case it prejudiced their opinion.

The case wrapped up after two weeks of testimony from unreliable witnesses, disputed evidence and a sequestered jury who had no idea what violence the O'Brien brothers were capable of.

One day shy of the thirteenth anniversary of Shauna's

abduction, after nearly seventeen hours of deliberations, the jury returned with a verdict. Shauna's family sat quietly in the courtroom, holding each other's hands, nervously awaiting the jury's decision. This was their one shot at justice for Shauna. If the jury declared the brothers not guilty, there would be no other trial. Across the room, Jim and Tim O'Brien casually chatted and chuckled with one another as they awaited their fate.

The jury filed in and the foreman gave their verdict. Both brothers were found guilty of second-degree murder, third-degree murder, involuntary deviate sexual intercourse, kidnapping and criminal conspiracy to commit kidnapping. They were found not guilty of first-degree murder and rape.

The brothers showed no emotion as the verdict was read, but Shauna's family celebrated quietly, hugging one another with tears in their eyes, grateful that their thirteen-year ordeal was finally over. Not only had they endured the agony of not knowing who killed Shauna, they had been the subject of judgment, suspicion and doubt themselves.

When it came time for Judge Oliver J. Lobaugh to hand down the sentences, he wasn't taking any chances. He was going to make sure the O'Brien brothers would never be released, even if there were a change in the law. The judge said to the brothers, "The world was a better place because of Shauna and the world would be a much better place without you walking free ever again."

When reading the sentencing remarks, the judge said:

 The conduct of the Defendants far exceeded the means necessary to commit these two crimes. The victim did not have to be killed and this was done in an attempt to cover up the terrible things that had been done to her and to prevent her from identifying her abductors/captors and the perpetuators of these crimes. The throwing of this young victim from a railroad trestle inflicted upon this young child a terror and a horror that went far beyond a typical violation of Involuntary Deviate Sexual Intercourse and Criminal Conspiracy to commit Kidnapping. What extreme cruelty it was to throw a child who was alive off the trestle onto the rocks below. What a horrific way for anyone to die, especially a young child. The evidence in the form of photographic autopsy evidence demonstrates the ripping of the victim's genitalia that clearly shows a cruelty that is not necessarily a typical part of these crimes.

These crimes had a devastating effect upon the victim's family, the citizens of the city of Oil City and all the members of our surrounding communities. Following Shauna's abduction and the finding of her battered and broken body, fear gripped our community. Citizens changed the way they went about their day-to-day activities; youth activities were restricted and even eliminated, and this effect continued for more than a decade, especially in Oil City.

We find that both defendants have

demonstrated absolutely no remorse for their despicable conduct. We find that both Defendants are extremely dangerous predators and we need to protect society from both of them as long as possible.

"Therefore we have imposed consecutive sentences in this case in the event there would be some change in the law which would make them eligible for parole on the charge of Second Degree Murder. We certainly believe that any lesser sentence would depreciate the seriousness of these crimes and their disastrous effects."

THE NEXT DAY, Ted Walker filed a motion to withdraw his plea to third-degree murder and kidnapping. Nobody believed anything he said. He was given the maximum sentence of twenty to forty years. He is expected to die in prison.

ON OCTOBER 27, 2005, the final candlelight walk and vigil took place. Those who were unable to attend the walk but who wanted to honor Shauna's memory were asked to turn on their porch lights at the time of the walk. Shauna's family was there, but there were no tears this time.

There would be no more candlelit walks. It was time for the town to heal

HEALING

T hree years later, Oil City took the final step in healing from the devastating crime that had defined their town.

A shaking Elizabeth Roess, supported by her mother and grandmother, fronted up to the council meeting and bravely read out her list of reasons why the council should reinstate Halloween. She pointed out that Halloween decorations are best appreciated at night and many people aren't home during the day to give out candy.

Elizabeth lived on the same street as Shauna Howe. Her parents remembered well the terror that gripped the town for thirteen years. But they and the teachers at Seventh Street School, the same school that Shauna had attended, encouraged Elizabeth and supported her petition.

The council vote was unanimous. It was time to put the tragedy that had defined Oil City for nearly two decades behind them. The ban on nighttime trick-or-

treating would be lifted, effective at the very next
Halloween. It was time to move on.

On October 31, 2008, Oil City eagerly anticipated the
return of a celebration that an entire generation had
missed out on. The excitement was tinged with sadness
and fear. The local radio station ran a campaign urging
parents to accompany their children and examine candy
before kids ate it. Double the usual number of police
were on duty that night. Many people felt a dark sense of
foreboding about the return of Halloween.

That night, children dressed in every costume imaginable ventured out onto the darkened streets of their own
city for the first time in their lives. Under the watchful
eyes of their parents, they went from door to door and
neighbors and strangers alike showered them with candy.
The night went without incident. Halloween had finally
returned to Oil City.

NOWADAYS, Oil City's population is still in a slow decline
but there are active attempts to revive the town's fortunes
through tourism, nature walks, heritage-listed oil sites,
and showcasing the beautiful historic buildings and
Victorian architecture. Shauna's schoolfriends have
grown up. Some have children of their own, others have
moved away. Those two terrible murders in the 1990s
continue to cast a shadow over Oil City's Halloween celebrations. Those who were around still remember it like
yesterday. Every year on October 31, without fail, a group
of Oil City residents pause and remember another little
girl who loved Halloween: Shauna Howe.

PART II

SIAN KINGI (AGE 12)

A TERRIFYING ENCOUNTER

On November 11, 1987, twenty-four-year-old retail assistant Cheryl Mortimer had a terrifying encounter. Upon driving out of a shopping center parking lot in Ipswich, twenty-five miles southwest of Brisbane in Queensland, Australia, she was flagged down by a middle-aged woman near the exit. Cheryl slowed down, assuming from the gestures the woman made that she needed help with directions. Pulling up beside her, Cheryl rolled down her window and was startled when a younger man sprang from nowhere and reached through the gap, grabbing her keys from the ignition. Once her car was immobilized, the man pulled out a knife, which he pointed at Cheryl's throat. Her assailant was so agitated that he cut his own hand, smearing a bloody fingerprint on the window, but before he could make whatever demands he had in mind, the terrified young woman was saved when a colleague approached the car. The couple abandoned their attack and took off in their own vehicle, a white station wagon.

Shaking and scared the couple might return or follow her, Cheryl drove straight to the police station to report the incident. She provided a detailed statement, including a description of the car and her best recollection of the license plate, which she believed to be LLE 439. She described the woman who flagged her down as middle-aged and hefty, with burgundy hair, and her companion as a scrawny younger man, perhaps in his late twenties or early thirties.

Ipswich police tracked down the owner of the license plate, but it turned out to belong to a Toyota Corolla owned by a person in a neighboring state, who had been nowhere near Queensland that night. Cheryl must have recalled incorrectly.

Determined to find the person behind the assault on his turf, Detective Constable Graham Hall of the Ipswich Criminal Investigation Branch ran a small notice in the local newspaper. To his surprise, two more women came forward with stories of similar frightening encounters with a man in a white station wagon, the day before Cheryl's assault. Both women were nurses from Ipswich General Hospital and the incidents occurred in the hospital parking lot. One nurse had locked her doors and driven away as the man banged on her window. The other, Nicole Close, had been coaxed out of her own car to provide the man directions on his map. She became spooked when he moved far too close to her for comfort and she spied hessian bags and ropes in his back seat. It was only when another hospital staffer came past the car, startling the man, that Nicole took the opportunity to jump in her car and get away.

Nicole thought the license plate on the man's car had

been LLF 429. Again, a search on the registration came up blank. There was obviously a creep hassling young women in the area, and detectives didn't plan on giving up, but they had little to go on. They started trying different combination of the letters and numbers provided by the women to see if any matched a white station wagon, but the detectives knew it was a long shot.

A STRANGER ON THE BEACH

Friday, November 27, 1987 was a warm spring day. The mid-seventies temperature was typical for Noosa, an idyllic coastal retreat on the Sunshine Coast, less than ninety miles north of Brisbane, Queensland. Before it was renamed Noosa Heads in 1988 and became a playground for cashed-up holidaymakers lured by its perfect weather and pristine beaches, Noosa was a quiet, safe town populated by retirees seeking a warmer climate and young families seeking to escape the big city for a more laid-back lifestyle.

The Sunshine Coast was living up to its name. It was warm enough that thirty-one-year-old bartender Elizabeth Young and her friend Bill Wallace had decided to spend the afternoon swimming at Castaways Beach, around four miles south of the township. Elizabeth was sunbathing after lunch when the black Labrador she had brought along started growling at someone walking along the beach. Elizabeth looked up to see an unshaven man in his thirties. His sun-bleached hair was typical of the area, but his scruffy KingGee shorts and work shirt were out of place on the beach in early summer. She thought she had seen him the previous day, too, looking similarly disheveled—perhaps even drunk—and figured he was a stranger to the area. She waved and called out a greeting, but the man did not respond. Instead he gave her an unwavering, cold stare which, along with the reaction of her usually placid dog, made the hairs on the back of her neck prickle with alarm.

Elizabeth was relieved when Bill emerged from the surf and joined her on the sand. Upon seeing her friend, the man resumed walking among the dunes, and the couple noted that he walked with purpose, as if searching for something. When Elizabeth told Bill about the odd encounter, he urged her to return to the beach parking lot. Bill's car had been broken into while parked there a couple of times lately, and he wondered if the stranger might be responsible. Bill's utility vehicle was still locked and nothing had been taken, but Bill didn't like the look of the only other vehicle in the parking lot. It was a white dust-covered Kingswood station wagon with a black-and-white license plate that meant it was registered out of state. Suspecting the strange man who had frightened Elizabeth was up to no good, Bill wrote down its number plate on a scrap of paper before returning to the beach, moving to a spot where they could keep an eye on activity around the parking lot.

The man hopped into the Kingswood and drove away around 3 p.m., towards Noosa Junction, through the shops, in the direction of Pinaroo Park. The incident had unnerved Elizabeth, but she and Bill agreed that you couldn't go to the police to report someone walking along the beach, no matter how strange he appeared.

LATE FOR DINNER

That same afternoon, Lynda Kingi and her daughter Sian had stopped at the bakery after school to get bread for the weekend. They had been shopping at Noosa Fair. Sian had ridden her bike straight from school to meet her mother, who had agreed to help her find the perfect material to make into a skirt for a birthday party Sian was attending on the weekend.

Twelve-year-old Sian Kingi was excited about Sunday's party. She was popular among her Year 7 classmates at Sunshine Beach School, and loved to socialize and dance. At school she enjoyed jazz ballet and was on the netball team, her 5' 6" slim frame giving her a significant advantage over other girls her age. Her dead-straight, long blonde hair came from her mother, but she had the olive skin and enormous dark eyes of her Maori father, making her a particularly exotic beauty. Teachers found her quiet and well-behaved, and she charmed everyone she met with her sweet, shy nature and good manners.

Their mission to buy material was successful, and at around 4.45 p.m., Sian told her mother she would go on ahead so she could change out of her school uniform, a summery dress of blue-and-white vertical stripes. Lynda would take the shortcut home along the sandy path, while Sian would take the longer route, riding on the bike track around Pinaroo Park. Sian slung her olive-green school backpack over her shoulders and set off on the path she'd taken a hundred times before. With her head start, she should easily beat her mother home, despite the extra distance.

Noosa in the 1980s was a country town on the beach. Nobody thought twice about letting their children walk to and from school or ride their bikes around visiting friends and playing in the park until it was time to come home for dinner. Lynda Kingi didn't hesitate in agreeing to Sian making the short bike ride as she selected a loaf from the hot bread display. The transaction only took a couple of minutes, and then Lynda walked the sandy track to the family home. When she arrived, Sian and her bike were not there. Lynda didn't think much of it, assuming the popular girl had run into some friends on the way home and stopped to chat about school or the forthcoming party.

It wasn't until dusk fell that Lynda started to become annoyed that Sian had not come home yet. Sian was not prone to disobedience or thoughtlessness, and it was surprising that she had stayed out so much longer than she had meant to. Nonetheless, she was well on the way to becoming a teenager, and that would no doubt come with some challenges when it came to curfews and deadlines. Lynda knew most of Sian's friends, and began ringing around to find her wayward daughter. With each response confirming that the girls had not seen Sian since she left school, Lynda became increasingly uneasy.

Lynda's husband, Barry, came home a little after 8.00 p.m. and the two immediately set off to Pinaroo Park to retrace the route Sian would have taken. The track went from behind the brightly-lit, busy shopping center through picturesque, quiet parklands of the reserve. It took them only minutes to find Sian's bike, her number-one prized possession, lying on the side of a path. They called out, but there was no response, nor any sign of Sian. Trying not to panic, but knowing that there was no way their daughter would have willingly left the bike behind, they threw it in the back of Barry's ute and headed straight to the police station.

SEARCHING FOR SIAN

When the couple walked into Noosa Heads police station at 8.40 p.m. and shoved a photograph of their daughter under Detective Sergeant Bob Atkinson's nose, the policeman immediately took them seriously. Noosa was a close-knit town with fewer than 15,000 residents and Atkinson, father of a teenage daughter who played in the same netball league as Sian, knew her by sight. The distraught parents quickly recounted everything they had done to locate their daughter before coming to the station. Even though Sian had only been missing a couple of hours, when the Kingis assured him it would be completely out of character for her to run away or take off to be with friends late at night, he sprang into action.

The police accompanied the Kingis back to Pinaroo Park to check whether Sian had somehow injured herself and had fallen somewhere unconscious, but it didn't take long to confirm that Sian was not there. Detective Sergeant Atkinson feared the worst. Upon returning to the station, he rang the night desk of the local newspaper, the *Sunshine Coast Daily*. Despite being past the deadline for submissions, the newspaper agreed to run a photograph of Sian and details of her disappearance in the Saturday morning edition of the paper. Sian Kingi, twelve years old, was officially a missing person.

Barry and Lynda Kingi spent a sleepless night, having called or visited every one of Sian's friends. The hours passed with agonizing sluggishness as they waited anxiously for daybreak, when they could resume their enquiries around town, aided by the news release that Detective Sergeant Atkinson had managed to get into the paper. By the time the sun came up, every available police officer in the district was on the lookout for Sian Kingi.

After the newspaper hit the streets and the story began to be passed around the community, the leads started trickling in. Some people reported seeing Sian in the park that day. A couple of people reported having seen strange cars, one of them a dirt-covered, white station wagon in a parking bay at the edge of the reserve around the time she went missing. Police officers dutifully took down every word, careful not to miss any detail that might help them.

Sian's disappearance made the Sunshine Coast news that evening. The next morning, the day Sian was supposed to attend the birthday party she had been so excited about, there was still no sign of her. That afternoon, the Noosa police department put in a call to Brisbane's Homicide Squad and asked for as many detectives as they could spare to make the trip up the coast.

By that afternoon, every local news bulletin was leading with the disappearance of Sian Kingi and leads came flooding into the Noosa police station. As often happens, many of them went nowhere. Some were observations or incidents that were unrelated to the disappearance, others were the product of overactive imaginations or even invented for attention. But one thing kept coming up: the station wagon with out-of-town plates. The reports differed on the details—some said it had curtains, others could see inside; it may or may not have had a roof rack. But it was always a dirty, white station wagon, probably a Holden Kingswood, several years old. Those who had seen its occupants provided a description of a surfie-looking man and a plump woman, but no little girl.

The people of Noosa and the surrounding district banded together like they never had before, united in the quest to find young Sian Kingi as fears for her safety grew. Detective Sergeant Atkinson took the Kingi family under his wing, personally ensuring they knew every step taken in the investigation.

That night, Lynda and Barry Kingi appeared on the TV news imploring anyone with any information whatsoever about Sian to contact police. Police urged everyone in the district who had a vehicle that even vaguely matched the description of the white station wagon to come forward so their car could be struck out of the investigation. They soon discovered that white station wagons were exceedingly common.

THE WHITE STATION WAGON

E lizabeth Young, the bartender who had been at the beach the afternoon Sian disappeared, was shocked to see Lynda and Barry Kingi on the TV on Sunday night. Having worked the night before and slept most of the day, she had missed the escalating drama captivating the town. Elizabeth and Lynda had worked together at the Mango Tree cafe a few years earlier, and Sian and her younger brother used to come in after school, enjoying iced coffees and milkshakes while they waited for their mother to finish her shift. Elizabeth watched with horror as the tearful couple held up a picture of the missing twelve-year-old. When the detective mentioned the dirty, white station wagon, Elizabeth picked up the phone and reported the man she had seen acting suspiciously at Castaways Beach the afternoon of Sian's disappearance.

It didn't mean much more than just another white Holden to check out among the thousands, but Eliza-

beth's story was specific enough that the police had her
come in personally to make an official report. The information Elizabeth gave them was one of the strongest
leads yet. They also asked her friend Bill Wallace to
attend the station as soon as possible in case he remembered more details.

By the next day, Monday, the search had intensified.
Police divers were ordered to prepare to comb nearby
creeks, and detectives added aerial searches to the pave-
ment pounding that had been relentless since Sian's
disappearance. Brisbane police had come through with
about a dozen detectives converging on the township to
offer their assistance, and a situation room was set up and
staffed around the clock, so that anyone who remembered something could come forward. A mannequin
dressed in Sian's school uniform was set up near where
she was last seen in the hope it might jog somebody's
memory.

That morning, Bill Wallace came into the police
station, having been urged by Elizabeth to tell them what
he remembered of the man and the car at Castaways
Beach. His description of both matched perfectly with
the information the police already had. But Bill had one
more thing. He had kept the scrap of paper with the
license plate number: LLE 429. Police ran the number
through the Queensland registration system, but there
were no cars that matched. Next they tried neighboring
New South Wales, but that also came back blank. When
they plugged the number into the computer database of
Victoria, over 1,000 miles away, it returned a hit. A Mrs.
Valmae Faye Beck of Mooroolbark, Victoria, owned a 1973

Kingswood station wagon with that registration. Her name went into the mountainous pile of the leads the police had to check.

BECK AND WATTS

Valmae Faye Beck, born August 2, 1943, was born into a life of disadvantage and dysfunction. Her unpleasant childhood was dominated by a cold and unloving mother who offloaded the girl onto any relatives who would take her, with little regard to how they would treat the young Valmae. Her three brothers ran wild and were not protective of their little sister, subjecting her to abuse instead of love. If no relatives were available, Valmae was left with strangers, some of whom sexually assaulted her. By the time she was twelve, Valmae's mother pulled her out of school and sent her to work in a clothing factory so she could pay her own way. In 1959, at the age of fifteen, she was registered as a neglected child and committed to the care of the state.

Between 1961 and 1972, Valmae was in and out of prison on a variety of offences, including theft, false pretenses, indecent behavior, obscene language, forgery and vagrancy. She changed her name periodically and drifted from job to job, working as a housekeeper, in a bar and as a cook, the latter after a stint in prison in Townsville where she did a cooking course. It was the only sort of work she ever got any pleasure out of.

Uneducated, unattractive and unlikeable, Valmae nevertheless managed to marry twice and gave birth to six children from at least two men, but probably more. She did little to improve on her own mother's parenting skills and her children either were taken away from her by the authorities and made into state wards, or taken by their fathers. Her second husband returned to his native Italy, putting as much distance between he and Valmae as he could, and taking the two youngest children with him.

Valmae spent much of her time in bars, gravitating toward the seediest pubs, run by staff who allowed her to keep drinking long after she should have been cut off provided she was able to pay. Her diet consisted of Chinese food and toasted sandwiches, and chocolate whenever she could get her hands on it. By 1983, she was an unhealthy, foul-mouthed drunk, estranged from her children and grandchild, living in one of the down-and-out suburbs of Perth, Western Australia, spending all her time and money on cheap drinks, lemon chicken and fried ice-cream.

It was in this state, and in one of those pubs, in the days when she went by the name Valmae Forte, that a mutual friend with underworld connections introduced her to Barrie Watts. Watts had an equally disturbing childhood and, as a career criminal with a sadistic streak, was also no stranger to the prison system. Although he was a decade her junior, Valmae and Barrie started a relationship that was punctuated by verbal and physical abuse. Valmae was loud and pushy, but the skinny, heavily tattooed, rodent-like Watts didn't mind resorting to violence and verbal abuse to keep her in line. Valmae was desperate to hang on to the one man who seemed willing to have a relationship with her. The two soon fell into a habit of full-day alcoholic benders, drinking in squalid dive bars until they were kicked out, and then carrying on in a local park until they passed out, only to wake and do it again the next day, a sordid, destructive kind of Groundhog Day.

They bonded over stories of their time in prison. Valmae had done time in Queensland and Western Australia and had changed her name several times to avoid the authorities. Valmae told Barrie about a woman she had been in prison with in Western Australia. Catherine Birnie was serving time for the abduction, rape and murders of four women with her partner, David Birnie. Catherine allegedly told Valmae that having sex while murdering a female was the greatest thrill of all. Barrie Watts listened to the story with great interest.

They got married on December 19, 1986, in Perth. Valmae was forty-three and Barrie was thirty-three. Valmae took the surname of Barrie's adoptive father, Roland Beck, a parson who had raised the orphaned Barrie in Fiji, before moving to Melbourne.

Theirs was not your average married life. Watts kept a large pornography collection, all of it featuring teenagers or actresses that looked like teens. He compared overweight, old Valmae with the never-ending parade of young girls in his videos and magazines who seemed willing to participate in all manner of activities with older men. Whenever Valmae baulked at doing something Barrie demanded of her, he threatened to leave her for someone younger and slimmer, feeding her insecurities. She watched the videos of the nubile young teens seething with jealousy, but also with a fascinated sense of voyeurism.

Even if they had been able to find work with their extensive criminal records, neither Valmae Beck nor Barrie Watts were able to hold down jobs, thanks to their alcoholism and antisocial behavior. They turned to crime and social security fraud to fund their drinking binges. A few months after one of his stints in prison, Barrie hooked up with an old accomplice with whom he carried out burglaries and at least one armed robbery. Barrie broke into cars to grab spare change, and when he found bank passbooks, he gave them to Valmae, who practiced copying the signatures until it was a close enough facsimile that she could withdraw money from the bank accounts.

By 1987, both Valmae and Barrie were out on bail on charges that, given their criminal histories, would most certainly carry lengthy jail sentences. Perth had become too hot for them, so they fled from the state and set out in their small sedan on the 2,000-mile trip to the opposite side of the country, where Barrie Watts' adoptive father lived in the suburb of Mooroolbark, around twenty miles from Melbourne. There they swapped the old sedan for a 1973 Kingswood station wagon, a car big enough for the two of them to sleep in when they were on the road. Valmae registered it in her name, using her father-in-law's address. Knowing that the police would soon come knocking on the door of Barrie's father asking about the two fugitives wanted on outstanding warrants issued by the Western Australian police, they didn't want to spend too long in Melbourne. In any event, Valmae hated city living and Melbourne was cold. It was not long before they headed aimlessly up north. They had no plan for where they would stop, but they preferred the warmer climate. After a rambling trip that took them through New South Wales and over the Queensland border, the dysfunctional couple settled in Lowood, a small town on the Brisbane River, forty miles west of Brisbane, where they rented an A-frame house on an acre block.

Barrie's obsession with younger women had not abated. They did not yet have a video player in the new house and he had left his porn collection behind, so he would go outside and perve on teenage girls walking home from school in their uniforms. Locals noticed that the new neighbor kept approaching teens in a way that was creepy, but nobody wanted to rock the boat by informing the police. Valmae felt increasingly threatened by his fixation with younger women, and Barrie was happy to play to her insecurities and paranoia that he would leave her, just as her other two husbands had.

Barrie Watts harbored fantasies of having sex with a young virgin, and he shared these fantasies with Valmae. When alcohol boosted his courage, he made Valmae drive to other neighborhoods and look for vulnerable young women to accost, with the intention of kidnapping them and forcing them into sex.

Around midnight on November 10, 1987, the couple cruised a hospital parking lot, waiting for any young nurses finishing late walking to a car in a secluded spot. They approached two of the nurses with a ruse of asking for directions, but one was immediately frightened and drove away, and they were interrupted before they could bundle the other into their car. The next evening, Barrie Watts made Valmae Beck wave down a car driven by a woman in her twenties as she left a shopping center parking lot near Ipswich. This time he got as far as pulling a knife, but was again interrupted by a passerby.

Valmae Beck became sulky and jealous about her husband's fixation on finding a younger woman to have sex with, but she went along with his clumsy abduction attempts. When she complained about his need to be unfaithful, Watts told her there was one way she could ensure his fidelity to her forever. If Valmae would help him find a young girl, young enough that they could be sure she was a virgin, he promised once he had had his way with her, the desire would be out of his system.

He wasn't fussy. He didn't care what color hair she had, or whether she was short or tall, she just had to be young, pretty and a virgin. Barrie told his wife that she just had to find someone who fit the bill so that he would know "I would be the first and last man she ever had." If Valmae helped him fulfil that fantasy, he swore to remain faithful forever.

A BODY IN THE WOODS

The week following Sian's disappearance was the busiest the Noosa police had ever experienced. The situation room was a hive of activity, with the community coming together and taking the police at their word when they said to report anything suspicious, no matter how minor. Every flasher, loiterer, pickpocket, drug dealer and suspicious-looking stranger found themselves being hauled into the station for questioning and sometimes found themselves being charged with an offence. However none of those reports led to Sian.

There was not a soul on the Sunshine Coast who did not know about the disappearance of Sian Kingi. Lynda and Barry Kingi were overwhelmed with love and support from friends and neighbors, kept constantly in the loop by Noosa police, and given free rein on the news networks to plead for their little girl's safe return. Police followed every lead, no matter how tenuous, and shared solid information with journalists so that it could be disseminated as widely as possible.

Sifting through the leads soon brought investigators to the report of the suspicious white station wagon and the odd behavior of the stranger at Castaways Beach. The car was registered to a woman with an address in Mooroolbark, Victoria, near the suburb of Croydon. Detective Senior Constable Alan Bourke, who had taken the report, called Croydon police station and asked detectives to check out the address.

The Croydon detectives soon came back with some interesting information. The address was occupied by an elderly man, whose adopted son, Barrie Watts, had recently visited from Western Australia with his wife, Valmae Faye Beck. Valmae had bought a white station wagon while she was there, using Mr. Beck's address for the registration. Not long after, the couple had headed off for Queensland. After calling their counterparts in Perth, police discovered that Barrie Watts had a record and was associated with another known criminal by the name of Valmae Forte, which they deduced was the previous name of Valmae Beck. Both were wanted on outstanding warrants. The police arranged to have their photographs sent by express mail from Western Australia to Queensland.

On the evening of Wednesday, December 2, eighteen-year-old Neil Clarke was watching the news, which as usual was dominated by the missing little girl, Sian Kingi. The urging from the police to report anything out of the ordinary, no matter how minor, triggered a memory of his walk home from his fruit-picking job that evening. He recalled being struck by a foul smell in the Tinbeerwah Mountain State Forest where he cut through to get to his home just on the edge of the woods. It was an odor he had never experienced before and it struck him that it could possibly be the stench of a corpse. He decided that if it he could still smell it when he was on his way to work the next morning he would have a look around, just in case it was something worth reporting.

Early the next day, Neil set off to his work in the orchard, taking his car to where he remembered the odor the evening before. The smell was still there. He'd never smelt a dead body before but he imagined it would smell like this. Neil stepped off the path and went a short way into the forest. What he saw sickened him to his core. He stumbled back to his car, drove straight home and called the police.

Detective Sergeant Bob Atkinson was in the situation room when the call was put through to him at a little after 9 a.m. Upon hearing what the young man on the other end of the phone had to say, he felt as if the wind had been knocked out of him. The room of dedicated detectives fell silent. Even though by now, nearly a week later, they suspected they were dealing with a murder, all of them had secretly harbored hopes that young Sian Kingi would be found alive and reunited with her frantic parents. Nobody doubted that the mutilated, decomposing body that Neil Clarke reported seeing on the banks of the creek in the forest was the missing schoolgirl. Atkinson took Detective Senior Sergeant Bob Dallow with him to the location described by the caller.

At 9.33 a.m. on Thursday, December 3, Queensland detectives Atkinson and Dallow found the body of twelve-year-old Sian Kingi, face up next to a shallow section of Castaways Creek. She was still dressed in her blue-and-white striped school uniform, pink socks and white sneakers. Her throat had been slashed and her face had started to decompose under the harsh sunlight to the extent it was almost unrecognizable. Her torso was covered in blood.

Bob Atkinson was a seasoned detective, but the sight made him recoil in horror. It was made all the worse by the fact that he personally had taken Lynda and Barry Kingi under his wing. Now he had to make the worst phone call of his life to the parents of a little girl who played netball with his own daughter.

THE ABDUCTION OF SIAN

On Friday, November 27, having spent the day drinking as usual, Barrie Watts told Valmae Beck, "Today is the day." The fantasy of sexually possessing a young virgin had swelled into an obsession. Fueled by alcohol, Barrie became fixated, determined to find a girl who would satisfy his perverted desires. The couple were in Noosa, 120 miles from their home in Lowood, and the warm weather meant there should be an abundance of girls swimming or sunbathing on the beach.

Upon reaching the Sunshine Coast, the couple began trawling the streets and beaches for vulnerable prey, but they couldn't find anyone who fit the bill. The women were too old, or they had friends or boyfriends with them. Boyfriends definitely ruled them out because Barrie needed someone innocent, so he could be sure that was her first. He was becoming increasingly frustrated and single-minded about his mission. The previous failures in the dark parking lots fueled his determination that today would be the day, no matter what. When he and Valmae fought, he stormed off on his own for a while, continuing his search on Castaways Beach, but he had no luck there. The one girl he checked out seemed spooked by him. He realized he needed Valmae with him, as young girls would be more likely to let their guard down around a motherly middle-aged woman than a scruffy thirty-something man who stank of alcohol. Valmae was grateful and relieved when he returned, forever paranoid that he would leave her.

As the day eased into evening, they still hadn't found their perfect victim. Pulling up at Pinaroo Park, Valmae tried to reassure her increasingly incensed husband that his fantasy would be fulfilled, telling him, "I got a really good feeling about today." She suggested they get out of the car to stretch their legs and walk around the park and as soon as they did, Valmae spotted an opportunity. A tall, blonde girl in a school uniform was peddling toward them on a bicycle, and apparently she was alone. Urging Barrie to duck from sight, Valmae plastered a look of concern on her face as the girl rode closer and motioned at her to stop.

When Valmae Beck waved down Sian Kingi and told her she had lost her dog, Sian dismounted immediately to help look for it, laying her bike on the edge of the path. There was no reason for the schoolgirl not to trust the grandmotherly type who was distressed at the loss of her little poodle with its cute pink bow. The lady pointed in the direction her mythical poodle had gone, off the path, and Sian peered into the thick bushes to see if she could spot the lost pup.

Before she had any idea that Valmae was not alone,

Barrie Watts sprang from his hiding place, and grabbed Sian roughly from behind, shoving a dirty cloth into her mouth to muffle her attempts to scream. He bundled her into the back seat of the Kingswood station wagon and held her down out of sight as Valmae jumped in the front and took the wheel.

As Valmae drove, Barrie bound Sian's wrists and ankles and gagged her with brown masking tape. The cloth stuffed in her mouth meant there was no chance of her making a sound. He never made any attempt to cover her eyes, nor did he disguise his face. He had no intention of ever letting her tell anyone what her abductors looked like. They drove about nine miles and turned down a secluded road through the state forest, stopping the car about one mile in. With the adrenalin pumping and alcohol coursing through his bloodstream, Barrie Watts was in a frenzy to carry out his sadistic plan.

Barrie pulled out a large bedspread from the back of the car, also letting out the couple's blue heeler, Rajah, and found a small clearing in the forest. He told Valmae to get Sian out of the car and remove the masking tape, being careful not to leave any marks on the girl, or disturb her long blonde hair. He wanted Sian neat and pretty, like the girls in his videos, who also wore school dresses. The school uniform was an added bonus as far as Barrie was concerned.

Valmae Beck spoke in a soothing voice to the young girl, telling her if she behaved that she would be all right and nobody would hurt her. She gently and carefully cut away the tape, taking extra care not to spoil Sian's hair, just as her husband had demanded. When Sian was free of her bonds, she followed meekly as Valmae led her to the bedspread where the vicious and drunk Barrie demanded she look at him and smile. Then he started to carry out his evil plan. For over an hour, Sian was subjected to unspeakable horrors as Barrie repeatedly raped and violated her. Perhaps distancing herself from the despicable acts being carried out against her, Sian was silent and obedient, just waiting for the nightmare to be over.

When he was finally finished, he told Sian to get dressed, which the terrified girl did, no doubt thinking her ordeal was over and she would be with her family again soon. Instead, once she was dressed, Watts ordered her to lie face down and told his wife to fetch him a belt from the car. Valmae brought him one of her own, but implored, "Can't we just leave her and go?" Barrie replied, "Don't be so fucking stupid. I can't trust her not to give me up."

Without another word, the psychopath placed his knee on Sian's back and put the belt around the little girl's neck. As it tightened, Sian finally made a noise, crying out "You're hurting me."

The sound of the girl complaining apparently enraged Barrie, because he took a knife from his pocket and slashed her throat. Then he rolled her over and stabbed her over and over again. Rajah, the blue heeler, became so excited that Valmae had to lead him around the other side of the car. Watts called out to her to come and help him as he finished the job.

At around 7.00 p.m., Barrie Watts dragged Sian's lifeless body a few feet off the creek bank into the bush. Meanwhile, Valmae Beck wiped down the murder scene and buried the little girl's underwear in the sand. On their way back towards the highway, they stopped briefly to throw the knife, tape, rope and belt, all wrapped in the bloody bedspread, into Six Mile Creek. Then they headed home, stopping only to pick up some milk and cat food on the way through Brisbane, arriving back at their rental in Lowood at 10 p.m. Valmae put their dirty clothes in the wash and started to cry. Barrie comforted her and told her not to be upset. He said that he didn't feel bad, that she did great and was a good wife. That night, the couple had sex together for the first time in ages.

FAREWELL SIAN

The discovery of Sian Kingi's body was a devastating blow for the entire Noosa community. Everyone had secretly hoped that, against the odds and everything they knew about the girl, the twelve-year-old had simply run away. Instead, a horror unlike any they had ever known had entered their idyllic town. Ever since Sian had gone missing, parents had become stricter. Children were no longer free to roam on their bikes until sundown or visit friends without being chaperoned between houses. With a deranged murderer on the loose, parents didn't let their children out of their sight and hugged them close more often.

The autopsy found that Sian had been raped, sodomized and stabbed twelve times in what appeared to be a frenzied attack. Some of the stab wounds occurred before her death, and others were postmortem. Her throat had been cut and three of the stab wounds had pierced her heart. One of her hands had almost been severed.

As Lynda and Barry Kingi prepared for their daughter's funeral, police redoubled their efforts to track down her killer. Detectives Atkinson and Dallow led the Homicide Squad team in sifting through over 700 leads, all of which had to be checked, even though most of them led nowhere. Many detectives worked around the clock, napping at the station, always on call. Some of them had children of their own and couldn't imagine having to deal with what the Kingis were going through. Their best lead was still the white station wagon, but they also had to field calls from clairvoyants who insisted on having their "visions" taken seriously, and mentally unwell people who confessed to the crime but could provide no more information than had already been printed in the newspapers.

Every white station wagon that dared to venture onto the roads was pulled over, many several times a day, and the drivers were aggressively grilled about their whereabouts the previous Friday evening. To save time, drivers who were cleared of any suspicion were issued with a card by the Brisbane police that stated they had already been questioned and their car inspected. They could flash this proof that they had been given the all clear if they were pulled over again.

The Kingis remained stoic and dignified, knowing they had to hold themselves together for the sake of their younger child, Sian's little brother. They expressed gratitude for the work of media and police, Lynda Kingi even bringing the overworked detectives dinner some evenings. Although devastated at the outcome, Lynda said she was grateful that Sian's body was found, because "We know she is at rest and nobody can hurt her anymore."

That weekend, the photographs of Barrie Watts and Valmae Beck arrived from Perth. The pictures were accompanied by a note stating that Watts had failed to appear in court on an armed robbery charge and Beck was wanted for a string of burglaries and obtaining money through false pretenses. Perth police did not know where they were. This news shifted the couple significantly up the suspect list and the investigators put out a bulletin to every police station across Queensland, describing the suspects and their car. Soon there would not be a detective in Queensland that did not have photographs of the people wanted for questioning over Sian's murder.

On Tuesday, December 8, five days after her body was found, family and friends gathered to farewell pretty, sweet, popular twelve-year-old Sian Kingi at a ceremony that brought together her Maori and Aussie culture. The sickened community mourned with the Kingi family, but many of them also seethed with a thirst for revenge. Led by Bob Atkinson, the Homicide Squad took a brief break to pay their last respects to the young girl. When they returned to the situation room, they had an urgent call to return.

CLOSING IN

When Detective Constable Graham Hall of the Ipswich CIB, 100 miles south of Noosa, saw the bulletin describing the white Kingswood station wagon and its registration number, he was stunned. The registration was one digit out from that supplied by Cheryl Mortimer, who had a knife pulled on her two weeks before Sian Kingi's abduction. It was also one letter out from that supplied by Ipswich General Hospital nurse Nicole Close. Neither woman had recognized the black-and-white license plate as one that was registered all the way down south in Victoria. While they had noticed it was an out-of-state plate, they assumed it had come from one of the states that more closely neighbored Queensland.

Detective Hall immediately called the investigators in charge of the murder, and contacted the nurses and shop assistant, asking them to come into the station urgently. All of the women identified Watts and Beck from a lineup of photos, and the bloody print left on Cheryl's car matched the fingerprints on file for Barrie John Watts.

Police were sure now that they had the culprits. They put out an Australia-wide bulletin in relation to the white station wagon, Valmae Faye Beck and Barrie Watts. The pair had already travelled thousands of miles in the previous weeks, from Perth, through Adelaide to Melbourne, and on to Noosa. They could be anywhere. Every police station in the country received a fax with details of the Kingswood, its license plate and mugshots of the suspects.

When the fax came through to Lowood police station, one of the young constables immediately thought he had seen the car locally. He had noted the Victorian license plates in his rear vision mirror when he was on patrol duty the previous week. It was unusual enough in a small country town to see an out-of-state vehicle that he had made a mental note of the first half of the number plate —LLE. Although he was due to knock off for the day when the bulletin came in, he put in a call to the Noosa police to let them know what he had seen.

On Wednesday, December 9, Detective Constable Graham Hall of the Ipswich CIB and a few of the detectives who had been working the situation room descended on Lowood. They were on the lookout for the most-wanted vehicle in Australia. It did not take long to drive the entirety of the town of less than 3,000 people and determine that it was not on the street or parked in public sight. The detectives began methodically combing the town on foot, asking every business owner if they knew the car or the couple. They visited every drinking hole, hoping publicans would recognize the alcoholic pair. It wasn't until the next evening that they had a breakthrough. A telephone service employee, Colin Harm, was having a drink at his favorite pub when the barman mentioned the intensity of the police questioning. Colin remembered seeing a white Kingswood station wagon with Victorian plates in the yard of a house near where he was working up a telephone pole. He'd been thinking of buying a similar model car, so had taken special note of it. He remembered exactly which house it was.

The next morning, Colin Harm led police to the A-frame house. The car was no longer in the yard and it looked like nobody was home, so police knocked on the doors of nearby houses. All of the neighbors recalled the car, because of the frequency with which the man of the house ·washed it, and they mentioned his creepy approaches to schoolgirls. When presented with a book of mugshots, the neighbors readily picked out both Barrie Watts and Valmae Beck. The local real estate agency confirmed that both their names were on the lease. That information was enough for police to obtain a search warrant for the house. Inside, they found hair dye packets in the trash and indications that someone had left in a hurry, but there was no evidence of any crime being committed. What they did find was a rolled-up newspaper on the kitchen floor. It was dated the previous Friday. Police had missed the fugitives by a week.

PSYCHOPATHS ON THE RUN

After they dumped Sian's body, Valmae Beck and Barrie Watts returned to their rented house in Lowood, confident that they had not been seen. Valmae dyed Barrie's hair brown and cut it very short, and bleached her own burgundy hair a white-blonde. They changed their clothing so they looked different from any descriptions provided by potential witnesses. They washed the car inside and out, so there were no fibers or hair from Sian in there. Barrie continued to reassure Valmae that he did not feel bad, and neither should she.

As the week wore on, they became more relaxed, until they heard the news on Thursday, December 3, that Sian's body had been found and that police were interested in speaking to the owner of a white station wagon. Spooked, the couple packed a couple of suitcases and headed back towards Melbourne, where they should be able to sell the car quickly for cash.

After crossing the border into New South Wales, and

needing to keep the car off the highways while police were looking for it, they settled into a motel in The Entrance, a scenic seaside town and popular holiday destination on the Central Coast, sixty miles north of Sydney. They practiced a story, fabricated by Barrie, that they would tell police if they were apprehended. It was a simple story: they had argued that day, Valmae had stormed off and Watts had driven to Noosa and slept for a couple of hours before returning to pick up his wife and take her home. Barrie had Valmae repeat the story back to him. Most of all, he impressed on her to never confess anything, nor to believe any story by the police that he had confessed unless she heard him with her own ears.

They planned to eventually return to the house in Lowood where their meagre possessions were stored once the media circus was over. Not wanting the hassle of an agent knocking on the door to collect unpaid rent, and perhaps raising questions about their absence, they sent through a money order to cover the payment. The couple had a lifetime of experience of evading police and holing up in small towns around Australia, where news of one interstate murder was less likely to get much attention on TV or the local papers. All they needed to do was lay low for a while.

LOOSE LIPS

etective Graham Hall became consumed with finding Barrie Watts and Valmae Beck. It was bad enough that they had accosted three local women, apparently with the intention to abduct them, but the knowledge that he had been so close with the license plate fueled him on. He had even had junior detectives trying different combinations and looking up the type of car those numbers were registered to, but the precise one, along with the right state, had eluded them. If only they had had the right information in time, Sian Kingi's murder might never have happened.

Returning to the estate agency responsible for the Lowood property, Detective Hall asked if they had any other information that might help. He was in luck. The real estate agent told the detective that a payment had just come in via a money order drawn at The Entrance. Hall relayed his findings to Detective Atkinson with mounting excitement. They had proof of Watts and Beck's whereabouts as recently as the day before.

The Entrance was 500 miles away, so Sydney police were notified. They acted swiftly, sending ten plain-clothes police into the small town. They didn't want to spook the couple and they certainly didn't want a shoot-out, which was a strong possibility, as Barrie Watts was known to carry a gun when committing his armed robberies. Within hours of descending on The Entrance, an undercover officer spotted the white station wagon leaving a supermarket parking lot. He followed it along The Entrance Road, where it pulled into a cheap motel on a busy intersection. The officer parked across the street and put in a call to the situation room, telling them that he had the suspect vehicle under surveillance. Detective Atkinson knew he had to be there for the arrest. The murder of Sian Kingi was more personal to him than any case he had ever covered. He was on the next plane to Sydney and then drove the sixty miles to the Tienda Motel.

At 5 p.m. on Saturday, December 12, with the help of a master key supplied by the motel manager, police burst in on Barrie Watts and Valmae Beck watching TV, surrounded by snacks. The couple offered no resistance and were arrested without incident for the attempted abduction of Cheryl Mortimer. Police brought the pair to local police station, separated them and launched into questioning them about the real reason they were there: the murder of twelve-year-old Sian Kingi.

Barrie Watts, seasoned career criminal, knew no good could ever come of talking to police. He refused to give his name and shook his head when asked whether the mugshot they had was a picture of him. He denied ever being in Noosa or being wanted in Perth, claiming to have just travelled up from Melbourne where he had lived for ten years. Valmae Beck, meanwhile, dutifully provided police with the story she had practiced after coaching by Watts, which placed the pair on the Sunshine Coast on the day of the murder.

When they were reunited in the police station, forty-four-year-old Valmae sat on the knee of her thirty-four-year-old husband as though she were a teenager, and the two smoked, kissed and chatted as if they hadn't a care in the world. When she was led away, Barrie Watts told his wife to stick by him. She promised she would.

The next day, Detective Atkinson escorted the pair on a plane back to Queensland and put them into adjoining cells in the Noosa lockup. Unbeknownst to the detainees, police had obtained a warrant to place electronic listening devices in their cells and they were monitoring and recording everything they said. Their conversations were taken down by hand by the officers listening to them, and transcribed again from the tapes, which picked up most, but not all, of what was said. The evidence they had so far was strong, but circumstantial, so police were hoping for the pair to incriminate themselves. Despite it being what they had rehearsed, Barrie Watts was angry at Valmae's statement that put them at the scene. Although they made some cryptic references to their activities, they said nothing police could use.

Detective Atkinson knew that they needed a stronger case than they had. He believed that they had a better chance of cracking Valmae Beck than her husband, who knew that keeping silent made police work a thousand times harder. Even though he felt sick even looking at the pair, Atkinson did his best to befriend Valmae. He told her about all the evidence they had compiled, building a damning case against her husband. He reassured her that he was sure she hadn't meant to do the little girl any harm.

Although Valmae stuck to the story she had rehearsed, every time he made her retell it, she added small details. As Atkinson lent a patient, sympathetic ear, Valmae Beck slowly began to break. She told Atkinson that her husband had an obsession with schoolgirls, and that after he picked her up again in Noosa, he had told her that she didn't have to worry about the obsession anymore. Latching on to her insecurities and concerns about her marriage, Atkinson gently probed, sympathized, and established a rapport with her. Just as he was wondering if he would have to build a case on the circumstantial evidence they had, she suddenly broke completely.

Valmae Beck began to talk, and once she started, she didn't stop for seven hours. She told Bob Atkinson her version of the rape and murder of Sian Kingi in excruciating, explicit detail. Right through the night, stopping only to drink water, go to the toilet or scoff down the chocolate she demanded the detectives bring her, Valmae Beck told and retold her story, adding the most minute observations and details about every despicable act perpetrated by her husband on the twelve-year-old girl. She described Sian's reactions and the expression on her face as Barrie did things nobody should have to endure. She relayed every word Watts had said, both to her and to Sian. Police who took her statement said that she seemed to relish talking about the sex acts carried out by her husband on the girl, almost as if she were narrating a sick, depraved porn film. By the time she had finished in the early hours of the morning, her statement ran to nearly thirty pages.

Most importantly, Valmae told them that she had cleaned up the crime scene, wrapping the murder weapon and items used in the kidnapping inside the blanket Barrie had used, and described exactly where she had thrown them into Six Mile Creek. A police crew was dispatched immediately. They soon retrieved the items, including the masking tape that still contained strands of Sian's hair.

On December 15, 1987, the day before Sian should have turned thirteen, Barrie Watts and Valmae Beck were formally charged with her murder. Valmae returned to her cell and told her husband that she had made a confession. She told him, "The only thing I didn't put in the statement was what happened between her and me. I just couldn't tell them that."

Barrie responded, "That's quite understandable. I'm glad you didn't."

He was taken aback when he was shown Valmae Beck's lengthy and incredibly detailed statement, but Barrie Watts remained tight-lipped with police. He knew that knowing what happened was one thing but proving it was another, and he taunted the police with this fact. However, Barrie couldn't stop himself from flying off the handle at Valmae for her betrayal when he returned to the cell next to hers. As soon as they were left alone, he growled through the wall, "You hung me; good on you, top wife… If you hadn't betrayed me, we could have got away with it."

Valmae responded, "No jury in the land would have found us innocent. You know it and I know it."

Barrie replied, "No-one saw us pick her up and throw her in the car, no-one seen her in the car, no-one seen us kill her. If you hadn't confessed, they didn't have a case." The bugs in their cell picked up every word.

Over the next twenty hours, the two incriminated themselves further and further. Valmae tried to convince her husband to plead insanity. She told him, "If you just listen to me, you will get out of it. I won't, but you will. I can't plead insanity but you can... You're off your tap... Going out and raping somebody is one thing, but to kill somebody in cold blood and not have any compassion at all, that worried me. It's been worrying me for weeks, since it happened. Because you told me it wouldn't bother you, but I thought it would."

Barrie responded, "I'd like to do it again." When Valmae protested, he said, "You wanted to as well. You wanted to do it again."

As Valmae began to regret her loose lips, the two discussed a suicide pact, to be carried out the following week, on the anniversary of their marriage on December 19. Eventually it came time for the two to be sent to separate prisons, where they were put among the general population.

Like many child killers, Barrie Watts did not have as easy a time in prison as he had when he was doing time for the more acceptable crimes of armed robbery, theft and break and enter. As his wedding anniversary approached, a correctional officer at the Brisbane Correctional Centre found him crying in his cell, claiming he was sick of being hassled for Sian Kingi's murder. When the officer pointed out he had to expect some harassment for that sort of crime, Barrie replied, "Yeah, but I didn't do it... I fucked her but I didn't hurt her." When the officer asked who killed Sian, Barrie Watts replied, "She did."

"Who's she?" asked the officer.

"Valmae Beck," responded Watts.

THE MOST HATED COUPLE IN
AUSTRALIA

Barrie Watts may have hoped that his wife would uphold her part of the suicide pact, meaning she would be unable to testify against him, but neither of them killed themselves. They did not see each other again until April 5, 1988, when they arrived at the Noosa Heads Magistrates Court for their committal hearings. They were greeted by a noose hanging from the court clock tower and hundreds of people with placards who had gathered to scream abuse at the suspected murderers. The parents of the Sunshine Coast had never encountered such evil before and, when the story came out, it dawned on them that it could just as easily have been any of their daughters who wandered across the path of these depraved psychopaths at the wrong time.

Although they seemed like a bloodthirsty mob, when the police who had led the investigation appeared on the steps, the mood suddenly changed. Someone called out for three cheers, and the crowd erupted into applause for the officers who had worked night and day to catch Sian

Kingi's murderers. At this time, when there had been much public condemnation of corruption in the Queensland police force, it was a ray of light for the police to have their hard work publicly acknowledged and to be appreciated for doing their jobs. The police involved in the investigation of Sian Kingi's abduction and murder were to be commended. Sexual murderers of children that involve abduction of a child by a stranger are notoriously difficult to investigate, as they are often carried out by someone who is not local and leaves the area immediately afterwards. Beck and Watts showed all the traits of serial offenders. The quick and thorough investigation by Queensland police almost certainly prevented further tragedies.

Valmae Faye Beck pleaded guilty to abduction and rape, and not guilty to murder. Barrie Watts pleaded not guilty on all charges. As the pair had turned on each other, they were committed to stand trial separately.

Valmae Beck's trial came first, in October 1988. The court heard Valmae's story of what happened to Sian Kingi in all its lurid, pornographic detail. It took ninety minutes to read out her statement, which was half an hour longer than Sian's actual rape and torture. Beck told the shocked and sickened court that Sian "never cried, never shed a tear, a brave little girl, she never uttered a peep, she just did everything he told her."

Although she painted herself as a passive observer, it was clear that she helped her husband kidnap the girl, despite knowing what he planned to do. The court heard the tape from the cell where she told her husband that she had left out "what happened between her and me," suggesting she may have been a far more active participant than she was letting on. Barrie Watts never made his own official statement to police, so there was nothing to contradict her version of the story. Valmae stuck to her tale that she was an unwilling participant, under the spell of the man she loved and would do anything to keep. She told the court, "I didn't feel I had the qualities to hold a man and I was terrified Barrie was going to leave me for a younger woman."

Nobody bought her story. At the conclusion of her trial, the jury took just three hours to find her guilty—not just of abduction and rape, but also of the murder of Sian Kingi. Prosecutors did not contend that she had performed any of the acts that killed the young girl, but her own testimony that Watts had said he wanted to be a virgin's first and last meant she must have known what was going to happen. Even knowing the likely outcome, she had willingly aided in her husband's crimes, even encouraged them.

On October 20, 1988, in the Queensland Supreme Court, Justice Kelly sentenced Valmae Fae Beck, whom he called "callous and depraved," to three years for abduction, ten years for rape and life for murder.

As a child rapist and murderer, Valmae Beck quickly became the most hated woman in Australia, surpassing even her friend Catherine Birnie. She was targeted by other prisoners, many of whom had children of their own and couldn't understand how a mother of six could do something so depraved to a child for the sake of approval from a man. Valmae had urine and feces thrown at her and spread around her cell regularly, and was bashed on several occasions, sometimes to unconsciousness. When she was seriously injured after being hit in the head with a tin can in a sock, she was transferred to a Townsville Correctional Centre for her own safety.

Valmae Beck represented the rarest of creatures—a woman who killed outside a domestic situation or her own family. According to an Australian Institute of Criminology report that came out a couple of years later, only eight per cent of female homicide offenders killed a person who was not known to them, compared to approximately seventeen per cent of male homicide offenders, and those situations usually involved robbery as a motive. Rape and murder of a random child victim by a woman was almost unheard of.

Barrie Watts went to court more than a year later, having pleaded not guilty to all charges of abduction, rape and murder. With no admission by Watts, the prosecution relied on the recordings of his conversations with his wife which, due to the terrible quality of the audio, may not have been sufficient except that Valmae Beck corroborated them. She became the principal prosecution witness against him. She had divorced him earlier that year, saying she regretted everything she had ever done with him. Her evidence was fundamental to the prosecution's case. Despite her so-called regret, she still seemed to relish providing detailed, specific descriptions of her husband's crimes to the court.

The trial lasted eight days. On February 8, 1990, after six hours of deliberations, a jury found Barrie John Watts guilty of the abduction, rape and murder of twelve-year-old Sian Kingi. The same judge who had sentenced Valmae Beck sentenced Watts to three years for abduction, fifteen years for rape and life for murder. Justice Kelly told Brisbane Supreme Court that the circumstances of the murder were so abhorrent that Barrie Watts' file should be marked "never to be released." To Watts, the judge said, "The vulgar crime shows you to be an evil man void of any sense of morality."

Barrie Watts fell squarely into the archetype of a sadistic–calculator murderer. These murderers inflict deliberate torture of their victims to obtain arousal. They will often approach their victim under a pretense, and before killing they beat, restrain and hold their victim captive, with brutal rape, often with elements of bondage involved. These offenders conceal the victim's corpse and enjoy reliving the act afterwards. Barrie Watts had an audience in his wife, to whom he bragged and reminisced about his crimes, but those who act alone will often write a diary or take mementoes from their victim.

There was great relief that it was unlikely the two would ever be released. Most Australians believed that their capture had avoided a potential serial killer situation. As McGregor said in an Australian Institute of Criminology study, "Barrie Watts and Valmae Beck only committed one murder before being apprehended. However, their "Modus Operandi" (MO) can be considered characteristic of the sexual serial murderer, with Watts openly admitting that he had intentions to commit further murders."

HARD TIME

That should have been the end of it: Barrie and Valmae rotting away in prison, never to be heard of again until their inevitable and welcome deaths. However, while he was in prison, Barrie boasted to other inmates about the murder of not only Sian, but at least one other girl. Hoping to close a cold case, Queensland police planted an undercover police officer in his cell, and investigators began to comb through unsolved abductions and missing persons in areas Watts was known to have been in.

One case in particular was the disappearance of thirty-one-year-old Brisbane mother and teaching student, Helen Mary Feeney. Helen had been studying to be a teacher at the North Brisbane College of Advanced Education at Carseldine. She had last been seen alive at 6.30 a.m. on October 29, 1987, at a caravan park in Brisbane's north, but she was not reported missing by her former husband until November 28, after she failed to show up for an access visit with their six-year-old son.

Helen had long been presumed dead, but her body was never found. Police came to believe that Barrie had killed Helen when she disturbed him breaking into her car in the grounds of the college where she was studying. The timing was right. It was not long before Sian's murder, when Barrie was hanging around places frequented by girls and young women.

Barrie Watts was put on trial for Helen Feeney's murder in 1995, and Valmae Beck once again testified against him. Valmae told the court that Barrie had told her that he had killed a woman and she later helped him dump the body, wrapped in a red comforter, at a rubbish tip near Lowood, where they burned it. However, no evidence could be found to corroborate her testimony, and police remained convinced that Helen Feeney was actually buried at another site and that Valmae knew where it was, but for some reason refused to tell them.

Police searched an area between Lowood and Wivenhoe Dam, where Valmae had shown them a shallow grave she said Barrie had dug for a woman the couple tried to abduct from a shopping center near Ipswich, but came up with nothing. Barrie denied any involvement, and the prisoners to whom he confessed were uncooperative with the court. Without a body, and with unreliable testimony from his former wife, Barrie was acquitted of Helen Feeney's murder. The undercover detective planted in the cell to befriend Barrie later suffered a nervous breakdown and resigned, attributing his collapse partly to the horror of working on the case and listening to the perverted ramblings of Barrie Watts.

In 1993, Valmae fell in love with serial rapist Robert John Fardon after meeting him at an annual barbecue put on for lifers. Their relationship lasted several years and by 1998 Fardon wanted to become her fourth husband, even asking a pastor if he could buy an engagement ring for Beck through mail order. They were denied permission and Robert was moved to a different prison. Their relationship appears to have stopped there.

At some point, Valmae converted to Christianity. Cold-case detectives periodically interviewed her about Helen Feeney and others in the hope that her newfound religion would spur her to tell the entire truth and help them find the body. She was also questioned about the disappearance of fourteen-year-old Sophie Helen Woodman, who went missing in 1980 after leaving her Perth home with a girlfriend to travel to the east coast. Police also suspected Valmae and Barrie were linked to the murders of twenty-year-old Sharron Phillips in Brisbane, and Adelaide girls Stella Mary Farrugia (nineteen) and Louise Bell (ten). However, if she knew anything, she provided no leads.

In 2003, Valmae Beck was in the newspapers again, this time for having befriended a One Nation senator, Pauline Hanson, who was serving time for electoral fraud. Hanson later told a women's magazine that she felt sorry for Valmae, with whom she had become friends after they "had a laugh and hit it off." The interview provoked the only public comment ever made by Sian Kingi's parents since her body was found. They were dismayed at the Ipswich politician's remarks, calling her obviously incapable of any clear judgment.

As twenty years in prison loomed, Valmae Beck tried several times to get parole, but was denied each time. In May 2007 she told Townsville Correctional Centre staff she had significant news to pass on in relation to Helen Feeney's disappearance, but subsequent questioning by investigators failed to result in any useful information.

By 2008 she was morbidly obese, weighing in at 330 pounds, was diabetic and had severe health problems. When she was hospitalized for minor heart surgery in May 2008, her condition deteriorated and she was put into an induced coma. Detectives who had remained convinced that she knew more than she was letting on about the murder of Helen Feeney and others, hoped for a deathbed confession. There was much debate about whether Valmae Beck, who had expressed a desire not to be resuscitated, should be kept alive for that reason.

Valmae Fae Beck died in custody at Townsville Hospital on May 27, 2008, aged sixty-four, from complications from heart surgery. She had served twenty years of a life sentence for Sian Kingi's murder. She never came out of her coma and investigators never got their deathbed confession. Any secrets she had died with her.

"Harsh as it may sound, and people may judge me on that, I don't think there will be many Queenslanders who would shed a tear in her direction and there would be some who would cheer," the acting Police Minister, Robert Schwarten, told reporters.

Bob Atkinson, now Police Commissioner, said that he was positive there were more victims besides Sian Kingi, Helen Feeney and the failed abduction attempts. He said to reporters, "Given the fact that (Beck and Watts) were so active, so ruthless, so organized, I find it difficult to believe that the only things they did were the ones we know about."

In 2009, at the age of fifty-three, Barrie John Watts

finally broke his twenty-year silence about Sian Kingi. He wanted to be considered for parole, which involves taking responsibility and expressing remorse for crimes committed. Barrie had not had a good time serving his life sentence for Sian's murder. When prisoners found him reading the court transcripts from Sian's trial, which included the perverse details of the crime supplied by his former wife, they attacked him, bashing him and sodomizing him with barbed wire. In an interview described by detectives as chilling, he admitted to the 1987 rape and murder of Sian. The detectives used the opportunity to try and get him to admit to abducting Helen Feeney, reminding him that, under Queensland's double jeopardy laws, because he had already been acquitted of her murder in 1995, he could never be charged again. A confession would provide her family with closure and she could finally be officially declared dead by the coroner. Barrie maintained his innocence, but the detectives believed that he only did so because he did not want to be known as a serial killer, which would adversely affect his application for parole.

His application was denied anyway.

Sian Kingi's murder changed the Noosa community. Children were no longer free to roam as they liked until dark. Those who were there at the time became more close-knit and more suspicious of strangers. Elizabeth Young never returned to Castaways Beach, but for many years after, on the anniversary of Sian's death, she wove plastic flowers through a swing set in the park where she was taken.

By the time Police Commissioner Atkinson retired in 2012, there was only one other case in his forty-four-year career that was seared into his brain enough to rival the rape and murder of Sian Kingi. As Police Commissioner, he oversaw the investigation into the disappearance and murder of thirteen-year-old Daniel Morcombe. Spurred on by the memory of Sian, he was instrumental in never allowing the police to give up on finding Daniel and bringing his perpetrators to justice, which finally happened after eight grueling years.

Barrie Watts remains in custody and has never confessed to any other murders or abductions. Those involved with the case have vowed to do everything in their power to ensure that he will never be released.

PART III

LEIGH LEIGH (AGE 14)

A PARTY INVITATION

On Friday, November 3, 1989, Robyn Leigh was peppering her fourteen-year-old daughter, Leigh, with questions. Leigh was going to her first late-night party for the sixteenth birthday of one of the local boys, Jason Robertson. It was mostly going to be students from Year 10 at her high school in Newcastle, 100 miles north of Sydney, Australia, but some of the younger girls had received an invitation too. Leigh was one of them, even though she was only in Year 8. This made her feel important and mature, as only a handful of girls her age had been invited.

On the other hand, Leigh's mother and stepfather, Brad Shearman, were apprehensive, particularly as the invitation said the party was an all-night affair, from 7 p.m. to dawn, and stipulated 'BYO', which suggested there would be alcohol involved. It was being held at an abandoned and semi-derelict building that formerly housed the North Stockton Surf Club, rather than at someone's home. But Leigh had been persuasive and she convinced them that the night could be viewed as a test. If Leigh behaved herself and was ready to be picked up at the stroke of 11.00 p.m., she would be given a bit more freedom to attend other parties and events. If she wasn't there at the allotted time, she would be grounded and banned from going to the upcoming dance at Newcastle High, which she desperately wanted to attend.

Robyn Leigh remained dubious, but she had always had an open and trusting relationship with her oldest daughter. Leigh Leigh's unusual name was a happy accident, rather than by design. She was born Leigh Rennea Mears, but after her parents' highly volatile marriage ended, her mother entered into a de facto relationship with a man whose surname was Leigh. The two had a child, a little sister for Leigh, whose name was Jessie Leigh. Leigh decided that she and her sister should share a surname and she loved the fact that taking her sister's name gave her the double-barrelled name Leigh Leigh. She liked the name so much she kept it after that relationship of her mother's also broke down.

In 1986, Robyn and her daughters moved to a house on Fullerton Street, Fern Bay, a working-class suburb in the Hunter region of New South Wales. Just south of Fern Bay lay Stockton. Stockton was technically a suburb of the city of Newcastle, but it was the only suburb that lay across the harbor mouth of the Hunter River, meaning anyone wanting to get there from Newcastle had to take a five-minute ferry ride or drive for half an hour. Its isolation from the larger town gave Stockton more of a provincial atmosphere: insular and close-knit. Many of its residents had an accompanying small-town mentality. The township was characterized by low incomes and high unemployment. It was here that Robyn met Brad Shearman. Brad moved into the house and became the girls' new de facto stepfather.

Leigh was a popular and outgoing girl and made friends easily at both Stockton Primary School and later at Newcastle High. By the time she was fourteen, she was an average student at school, with aspirations to become a veterinarian. She was relatively well-behaved in class, but sometimes exhibited a rebellious streak with her mum and stepdad, something that is not unusual among teens of her age.

That warm spring evening, Leigh was excited. There wasn't a lot to do for teens in the area. The discos that used to be held at the Masonic Hall had limped to a halt, and the local movie house had shut down. There were occasional gatherings at the old clubhouse on a Friday night, when the teenagers listened to the local band practice, drinking beer or cask wine acquired by an older sibling or friend. Otherwise, they all hung out at Roberto's Pizza Bar.

Leigh's social life until then consisted of going to the movies in Newcastle, roller skating, ping pong and hanging out with friends. Jason Robertson's sixteenth birthday party was her first real party and she was going with a couple of girlfriends. It promised to be a fun night out. Jason was a cool and popular surfie type and Leigh was secretly excited that another boy, who she had a crush on, would be there. He would be playing in Cardinal Sin, the band that was the entertainment for that night. She assured her mother that adult supervision had been arranged. She would know most of the kids at the party and she promised to be ready to be picked up by 11.00 p.m.

That evening, persuaded by her daughter's arguments and happy to see her so excited, Robyn dropped Leigh at Roberto's Pizza Bar, at 7.00 p.m. Roberto's was the only place in Stockton that had video games and it had become the favorite meeting and hangout spot for Stockton's teenagers. Leigh was meeting her friends at Roberto's and the three girls would walk the mile to the clubhouse where the party was being held.

Robyn waved Leigh goodbye, and reminded her to be ready to be picked up by her stepfather four hours later, or there would be consequences.

SEARCH FOR A TRUANT

Just before 11.00 p.m. that night, Leigh's stepfather, Brad Shearman, left the house to pick her up. Over an hour later he returned, agitated, without his stepdaughter. He told Robyn that she had not been at the agreed meeting spot and, annoyed, he had gone looking for her. Wandering through the clubhouse where the party was still in full swing, he was distressed and angry at the scene he found. Drunk teenagers were strewn around the building and on the beach, screaming and carrying on, in various states of undress and public displays of affection, vomiting in the bushes or passed out drunk in the gutter. There was no sign of the promised adult supervision, and after questioning a few partygoers, Brad had discovered that by "adult" they meant two boys aged eighteen and nineteen, who had been invited to act as bouncers for the event in return for a case of beer. Brad asked around about Leigh, but when he could get a coherent answer, nobody seemed to know where she was. Someone said she might have gone home early.

Brad drove home in case she had walked or got a lift there, but after telling Robyn what he had found, he headed out again. Robyn stayed behind in case Leigh and Brad had missed each other and Leigh was making her own way home. Brad drove around the nearby streets, before returning to the clubhouse where the party was winding up and spilling out onto the beach. There was still no sign of Leigh.

Becoming frantic and disturbed about the state of the party, at around 2.00 a.m. he returned home and grabbed his three-wheeled motorbike, which he could take over the sand tracks and around the dunes of the beach near where the party had been held. He told Robyn he searched every track and hollow he could find in the dark, but he couldn't find Leigh.

Finally, he returned home, assuming that she must have gone to a friend's place or fallen asleep on the beach somewhere. It wasn't uncommon for surf club parties to end on the beach and go on through until the next morning.

It was infuriating, because the next day was Jessie's sixth birthday and her big sister ought to be there when the little girl woke up. As far as Robyn was concerned, Leigh had failed her first party test. There would be no dance and she had a lot of explaining to do.

EVERY PARENT'S NIGHTMARE

The next morning, Brad Shearman resumed his search for Leigh while Robyn began ringing around the homes of her daughter's friends to find out if she'd had a sleepover. Brad headed back to the clubhouse, hoping the daylight would reveal Leigh's whereabouts. At around 9.15 a.m., he spotted some people standing less than 100 yards away from the clubhouse, talking animatedly as they stared at something on the sand below. Fearing the worst, he ran towards the little group.

What he saw was every parent's worst nightmare come true. Leigh's body lay naked, her legs spread apart and her face almost unrecognizable. She was still wearing her Dunlop Volley shoes and pink socks, but her underwear and shorts had been pulled down and were around her right ankle. The rest of her alcohol-soaked clothes were found nearby. One side of her skull had been completely smashed in and her face was covered in blood. There were bruise marks around her neck. She had been dead for some time before being found that morning.

Nearby was a thirteen-pound, bloodstained rock of concrete. Blood spatters were soaked into the sand up to ten feet away. Tucked inside Leigh's shorts pocket was the invitation to the party she had been so excited to attend.

The birthday boy, Jason Robertson, had found her. Jason had helped Leigh's stepfather search the night before, but it had been dark, which made searching on the beach and among the dunes difficult. He had received a call from Leigh's frantic mother telling him Leigh had never returned from the party and he had gone searching among the sandhills when the sun came up.

Newcastle police arrived shortly after, and the area was declared a crime scene. Police had known that there was a party on the night before and had done a drive-through inspection at around 8.30 p.m., when they claimed everything seemed to be in order. They immediately sought to identify every person who had been at the party, asking Jason to supply them with a list of invitees. The neighbors in the area said that the party had mostly been quiet, but one person told them they had heard screams from a girl and loud swearing by a man before everything had gone quiet.

Reporters descended on the scene and grabbed quotes from anyone they could. The *Sydney Morning Herald* spoke to two girls who claimed to be Leigh's best friends, but who had not been at the party. The newspaper quoted one as saying Leigh was "a very attractive girl which tended to make her the target of a lot of boys and we used to have to protect her." As neither had been there the night before, the girl surmised, "maybe she thought she could protect herself."

The newspapers reported that police believed Leigh Leigh had been raped several times in what might have been a gang rape. There might have been a hundred kids at the party that night. Surely someone had seen something. Surely the case would be solved in no time.

A TOWN UNDER SUSPICION

Over the next few days, police tried to piece together what had occurred the night of the party. One by one, over fifty teenagers were questioned at the station or at their homes about the events of the night. A picture began to emerge of a wild party with most attendees between thirteen and eighteen years old, but a couple as young as ten. There were also some runaway girls in attendance, who police later reunited with their families.

The investigation was hampered by what police came to call a "wall of silence." Most of the teens were reluctant to talk about anything that could get them or their friends into trouble, and many of the witnesses were affected by alcohol and drugs at the time of the events. Their recollections were impaired and some invented stories or flat out lied about being there. Some witnesses gave as many as three different accounts of key events. Police were also up against general distrust of police and silence among the boys of Stockton, who lived by a code of toughness and mateship. It was a well-established creed in rural Australia that a bloke never dogged on his mates, no matter what their crime.

It wasn't just Stockton's teenagers hampering the investigation. Few parents were interested in assisting police when it came to their kids and the insular township closed ranks. Those who knew didn't want to get involved and those who suspected thought it better to mind their own business. One middle-aged caller to talk-back radio said, "It's un-Australian to dob in a mate."

Bit by bit, police began to piece together the events of the night from kids who had to be reassured that nobody would find out that they had talked. Police ascertained that after Robyn had dropped Leigh off at the pizza shop, she had met with her girlfriends as planned, but they also met with an older friend who bought them a bottle of bourbon.

Leigh, excited by the prospect of her first real party and an inexperienced drinker, downed half the bottle mixed with cola, unaware how dangerous that could be. By the time she arrived at the party, she was already blind drunk, staggering and slurring her words. Nevertheless, this didn't stop the bouncer, Matthew Webster, from marking her arm in green Texta when she showed him her invitation and letting her into the clubhouse where the party was just getting started.

At around 8.30 p.m., the police, who knew about the party at the abandoned clubrooms, did a drive-through. The kids scrambled to hide their alcohol in the sandhills and police reported nothing amiss, other than a rowdy bunch of teenagers letting loose at a typical party.

Jason Robertson admitted there had been some

drinking, but claimed it was minimal and most of the booze had been taken by his older surfer mates. He said, "Leigh had a couple of drinks, but most of us were just drinking coke." It was the kind of lie teenagers told all the time and adults pretended to believe.

In the days after the party, police methodically interviewed fifty people on their list, and expanded that list as they received more information. They zeroed in on one incident that they thought might be key to the murder. Some of the girls at the party said that around 9.00 p.m. Leigh had left the clubhouse for a walk to the beach and may have been accompanied by a male partygoer. Leigh returned to the clubhouse a little while later, extremely agitated. She told a couple of her friends she had been raped and was worried about being pregnant, but she was such a drunken mess they didn't take her very seriously. They claimed they sat with her and asked her if she wanted them to call her parents, but she didn't, instead stumbling off outside.

The police were shocked at the attitude of the towns' parents, with few coming forward of their own accord. Detective Sergeant Lance Chaffey told reporters, "I'm looking at sixty suspects, but only two parents have bothered to contact us to assist us in what their kid might have seen." He theorized that some parents may have been feeling guilty for letting their kids go to that sort of event as Leigh's murder reflected on their inability to properly supervise their kids. Matthew Webster and Guy Wilson, the two boys who had been engaged as "bouncers" were only a couple of years older than most of the partygoers.

Many of the boys who had been at the party felt like they were under a cloud of suspicion for Leigh's murder and were being judged by some townsfolk. Police told reporters that everyone who was at the party was a suspect and that very few people had been eliminated. Everyone in town was looking sideways at anybody who was known to have been there. Jason Robertson complained he could barely leave his house because everyone was whispering and pointing at him, knowing that it was his party where the incident happened.

Matthew Webster, or "Fat Matt" as he was known, thanks to his 240-pound frame, was another who felt accusing eyes on him. He told a reporter who interviewed him a couple of days after the party, "The problem with Stockton is that there is nothing for us to do at night." So when a teenage party was on, everyone in town wanted to go and let loose. Matthew said he'd left the party early to go to the pub and get a beer.

Leigh's murder continued to attract media coverage. A couple of newspapers, looking for a fresh angle, ran stories about the prevalence of acquaintance gang rape in rural towns. The reports said such occurrences were more common than people realized, and much of the time the girl was held responsible for getting herself into that situation. Several girls were quoted as not reporting their rape due to shame and the fear of being blamed, especially if they had been drinking or taking drugs at the time.

Leigh Leigh had told her mother that she planned on being a virgin until she was sixteen years old. When her postmortem test results were returned, they confirmed that she had been a virgin before being assaulted that night. The tests also showed that she had been subjected to extreme sexual violence. She had vicious cuts, and bruising and sand was found deep in her vagina. She had been choked and strangled while she was still alive, but the cause of death was one of several blows to her head with the heavy rock.

A newspaper report on November 8, five days after the party stated, "Police believe Leigh was raped several times and that more than one person was involved," but were unsure whether the rape and murder were linked. However, some locals were questioning if a rape had occurred at all. After all, they reasoned, nobody seemed to deny that she had been drinking. Maybe she had "asked for it," the parents of some of the boys suggested.

"Yes, it's a terrible thing, but I hear she was a bit of a sleep-around," one resident told reporter Mark Riley.

WHAT HAPPENED AT THE PARTY

L eigh Leigh's funeral was held on November 9, 1989. Her distraught father, Robert Mears, returned to Newcastle for her funeral. Both he and Leigh's stepfather, Brad Shearman, were pallbearers.

The church was filled with friends of Leigh, mostly girls, who sobbed through one of Leigh's favorite songs, Cher's *If I could turn back time*. As always, reporters were there, looking for a new angle or new quotes to put in the local newspapers. Some of the younger girls told the reporters how scared they were walking the streets, knowing that there was a murderer on the loose.

After Leigh was buried, allegations and gossip flew around the town with increasing intensity. Fights broke out when some people thought that the code of silence had been broken. Fingers were pointed at partygoers who were suspected of talking to police. Nearly everyone in town had a theory about who had done it. Teenagers no longer hung out at Roberto's Pizza Bar.

On November 12, newspapers reported that there had

been new leads provided to police. According to that report:

> Detectives want to trace two schoolgirls who fought off attackers trying to abduct them the night pretty Newcastle schoolgirl Leigh Leigh was raped and murdered. Police believe there may be a connection between Leigh Leigh's brutal end and the attempted abduction. The schoolgirls managed to save themselves when a gang tried to drag them into a car about 3.00 a.m. on the morning of Saturday, 4 November.

Nothing came of that lead—it went into the pile of lies, half-truths and obfuscation that dogged the investigation. Meanwhile, police were putting together a more complete picture of what happened that night, and it was becoming progressively uglier.

Witnesses claimed that Matthew Webster, the eighteen-year-old hired to be a bouncer, had said to other boys at the party early in the night, "We're going to get Leigh pissed and all go through her." A fifteen-year-old boy, who can't be named for legal reasons, was also overheard saying, "I'm going to go and fuck her." For ease of relaying the story, the boy will be referred to as Cory, but that is not his real name.

Shortly afterwards, Leigh was seen staggering off to the beach with Cory. After the event, Leigh returned to the party crying, bleeding, obviously in a lot of pain and told her friends, "Cory fucked me. I hate him." She was hysterical and stumbling, still clearly feeling the effects of the bourbon. Blood was visible between her legs and witnesses said it was clear she was in pain.

One of the boys who was at the party later told police (as reported by ABC *Background Briefing*):

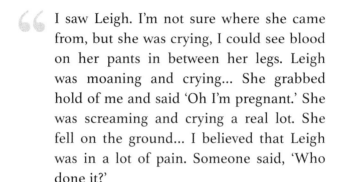

> I saw Leigh. I'm not sure where she came from, but she was crying, I could see blood on her pants in between her legs. Leigh was moaning and crying... She grabbed hold of me and said 'Oh I'm pregnant.' She was screaming and crying a real lot. She fell on the ground... I believed that Leigh was in a lot of pain. Someone said, 'Who done it?'

He said that Leigh had named Cory. Cory later told police that Leigh had instigated the walk down to the beach, as well as the sex that came afterwards.

Two of Leigh's girlfriends took Leigh away and sat her down at the table where they attempted to comfort her. However, she was too distressed and stumbled back outside bleeding, distraught and seeking assistance. The boys at the party, who had by now heard about the sex on the beach, crowded around her, laughed at her and called her a slut.

The party's other bouncer, nineteen-year-old Guy Wilson, assuming she was easy prey, also demanded sex from her. When Leigh refused, he shouted obscenities, spat on her and pushed her to the ground. A group of up to ten boys then gathered and stood in a semicircle around her as she lay in the gravel. Yelling abuse, they kicked her, spat on her, poured beer on her face and threw bottles at her cowering figure as she went into the fetal position.

One eyewitness told police, "I saw Leigh Leigh lying on the ground near the club with a group of seven or even more boys standing around her." The eyewitness named the boys and said, "These boys standing around Leigh were spitting beer on her and kicking her around the ears. They were kicking her pretty hard."

One of the boys who was standing over Leigh and participating in the abuse told police, "They all had twist tops in their hands, and they were pouring beer over her head and body and yelling abuse at her like, 'You stupid bush pig, slut' and things like that. I walked over to her and said, 'Get up you stupid bitch.' I laughed at her, but I didn't pour any beer on her."

Another of these boys told police, "While I was standing with them over Leigh, I heard Matthew say things like 'Get that into you, you slut' and 'Take that you slut.' Guy Wilson said the same things. Leigh just lay there the whole time, she did not say anything, but she was rolling around."

A girl who attended the party said, "These boys standing around Leigh were spitting beer on her and kicking her around the ears. They were kicking her pretty hard, but not as hard as they could have." Girls who attended the party were generally reluctant to speak, lest they be the target of the next round of rumors or targeted for an attack similar to what Leigh endured. It was a place and time that once a girl was branded a slut, there was no coming back. Boys would persistently badger them for the sex they believed they were entitled to and girls would shun and ostracize them, fearing that any association would tarnish their own reputation.

Another boy involved in the incident described what happened next. "Everybody had stopped pouring the beer over her and Leigh started to slowly get up and then staggered across the path and picked up an empty beer stubbie, we were all still laughing about the beer spitting when she threw the beer bottle at all of us, I ducked and I think the other blokes ducked but it didn't hit any of us."

Guy Wilson picked the bottle up and threw it at the retreating girl, hitting her on the leg. Leigh was said to later have returned and been subjected to even further abuse. The partygoers laughed as she sobbed and vomited. The band stopped playing during the commotion and one of the band members joined in, spitting his own beer onto Leigh.

One of the boys told police, "I saw Leigh come into the hall. And she came up to us. And we were calling her a slut, mole, bitch, and we poured beers over her and spat on her, and I pushed her with my hands, while I was doing it she was crying, and she got up and walked out."

The witnesses said that they had last seen Leigh Leigh staggering off toward the beach alone, in hysterics at around 10.15 p.m. The band went back to playing and the teenagers carried on partying. The boys never gave Leigh another thought other than to laugh amongst themselves about what had transpired, and the girls were just glad it wasn't them.

A WALL OF SILENCE

As these tales circulated the town, it was clear that there were many witnesses to Leigh's distress and that up to ten teenagers had directly participated in the humiliating assault. Parents told their boys to keep their mouths shut and spread their own version of events that Leigh had attended the party intending to get drunk and have sex with the boys there.

But police couldn't ignore the eyewitness accounts that matched each other's stories and the forensic evidence. By November 15, 1989, police had narrowed the list of suspects to a number of young people, but believed that Matthew Webster, Guy Wilson and Cory were the three most likely to have been responsible for her murder, or at least aware of who was involved. That day the three boys were picked up separately by police from the streets of Stockton and taken to Newcastle police station for questioning.

Cory was hanging around outside Roberto's when two police grabbed him and put him in the back of a police car. Matthew Webster had been sitting on a fence outside the home of a friend, Adrian, when two police officers approached and asked him to go with them "to clear up a few things" and that it would only take five minutes. He agreed to accompany them and walked with them the short distance to Stockton Police Station. Guy Wilson was on his way home from the Gladstone Hotel when he was approached by two or three police officers.

The three boys were questioned about the allegations against them about their conduct at the party and where they were around the time of Leigh's death. Cory and Guy did not have a specific alibi, claiming to just be hanging around the party, but Matthew said he had left the party early to go and drink at the local pub before meeting up with friends at Roberto's. The police soon established that this claim was untrue and Matthew admitted he had lied. He, too, had no real alibi.

The questioning led them to be charged with some minor offences relating to events that took place at the party. Cory was charged with sexual intercourse with a child between the ages of ten and sixteen and also with supplying hash. Guy Wilson and Matthew Webster were charged with common assault on Leigh both outside and inside the clubhouse prior to her murder, when Guy pushed her to the ground and they had both taken part in kicking her and spitting on her. Matthew was also charged with supplying cannabis to two teenagers.

Matthew Webster and Guy Wilson were kept in custody overnight and were bailed by the magistrate at court the following day for $1,000 and released to the care of their parents. Cory, being underage, was released in the early hours of the morning of that day into the custody of his mother. All three claimed that they were assaulted by police while in their custody during that period. Once those charges had been laid, the investigation seemed to be wound down.

Most of Stockton was hoping that the matter would die down and go away, seeing the incident as a tragedy that arose from "kids being kids" and a party that got a bit out of hand. But others kept the rage alive. Local resident Graham Parsons printed posters that featured a drawing of three long-haired male figures dressed in T-shirts and shorts with flannelette shirts tied around their waists, one clutching a rock, standing over a prostrate girl. Across the image he printed the words: "Shame Stockton Shame: Dob the gutless bastards in."

Graham later told *Background Briefing* that he lost a lot of faith in people when his community began "converting the truth into secrets." The posters were his attempt at breaking the code of silence that closed over Stockton in the days after the murder. He plastered them on telephone poles all over town.

By the end of the next day, every single one of them had been torn down. He never found out by whom.

ON DECEMBER 15, 1989, Matthew Webster pleaded guilty to the charges of assaulting Leigh Leigh and of supplying hash to two fourteen-year-old girls at the party, but denied any knowledge of events that occurred outside the clubrooms that night.

Guy Wilson entered no plea and his case was adjourned until January 19, 1990.

Cory pleaded guilty to sex with a minor, but alleged that it was Leigh who suggested "Let's do it." He was convicted and given a sentence of six months, which he appealed. At the appeal, the judge found that the sex had been by consent—despite the witness reports that Leigh had been so drunk she had barely been able to stand, and her obvious distress straight afterward. Cory's sentence was reduced to community service for unlawful carnal knowledge.

BOYS WILL BE BOYS

When news got around that the judge had found that the sex had been consensual, much of the town turned on the dead teenager. Her reputation was soon in tatters as gossip about her promiscuity raced around the community. People said she had brought it on herself because she had willingly drunk the bourbon that had been given to her.

In industrial towns in the 1980s, there was very much a "boys will be boys" attitude. If girls were raped by boys they knew, they must have deserved it or done something to bring it on themselves. People even began to blame the dead girl for ruining the lives of the boys who had been convicted of minor offences in relation to that night.

As rumors and theories swirled, suspicion came down heavily on Robyn Leigh's de facto, Brad Shearman. The whispers down the pub and at the school were that he had been sleeping with his stepdaughter for months. The townsfolk noted that he had been away for several hours claiming to be looking for Leigh. The story went that he had found Leigh walking along the beach after the party and, overcome with rage when she told him she had been sexually assaulted, his rage grew to violence and violence to murder. The rumor was told so often to police that Brad became a prime suspect in the murder of Leigh Leigh, despite a distinct lack of evidence.

The townsfolk began to turn on each other. Fingers were pointed, blame was apportioned and neighbor pitted against neighbor as police failed to close the case.

On January 28, 1990, a group of four boys spotted Matthew Webster in the street and taunted him about Leigh's murder. Matthew grabbed one of them and reportedly "went off his head," smashing the boy through a car windscreen, dragging him out again and thumping him repeatedly on the ground. He was fined $250 for offensive behavior.

Similarly, Brad Shearman was charged with assault after he confronted Guy Wilson and punched him to the ground. Guy had allegedly taunted Brad, telling him that Jessie, Leigh's six-year-old sister, would be next.

The abuse turned on Robyn as well, blaming her for moving into the area. If she and her family hadn't moved to Stockton, the whole ugly incident wouldn't have happened. Those poor boys were being harassed. Leigh got what she deserved. Still dealing with her grief and shock at her daughter's violent death, Robyn couldn't understand what she or her daughter had done to deserve the treatment. Eventually she took Jessie out of school because of the abuse she was getting from other students.

Somehow, Stockton had turned the narrative from a child being brutally raped and murdered to rage at a young girl they considered a worthless slut whose behavior had brought shame on the town and harassment to boys who were just being boys, and who had probably brought what had happened to her upon herself.

A CONFESSION

On February 16, 1990, police once again picked up their two main suspects, Matthew Webster and Guy Wilson. The two were interviewed separately, then placed together in another interview room that had been bugged by police. The police hoped they would incriminate themselves or someone else at the party, but they didn't say anything that helped the investigation.

Nevertheless, when they were again split up, Matthew Webster suddenly and unexpectedly made a full confession to the murder of Leigh Leigh. Police were stunned by this turn of events. Although Matthew Webster was one of several suspects, they had no hard evidence against him. It came out of nowhere.

Matthew said to the police, "Well I did it... but I just couldn't believe it happened it's just unbelievable... I went to look for my beers and I saw Leigh Leigh sitting down on the grass and my beers weren't there. Somebody must have pinched them. And then I walked up to Leigh

Leigh and she carried on with her normal shit and I tried to get on to her. Then we walked down to the bushes, and I pulled her clothes off and I pulled my shorts down and I put my finger in her pussy. I thought I was right for a root [Australian slang for sexual intercourse], and then she started pushing me away saying, 'Don't.' I lost my temper and I did what I did."

When the police officer asked him to elaborate on what he meant by "Did what I did," Matthew said, "She was punching and pushing and I grabbed her by the throat and she said *Don't* and I choked her a bit. She stopped punching and I grabbed the rock, and killed her."

He reportedly said in his admission, "I am just so, so, so sorry. I would do anything to go back in time so it would not happen. I feel like a c_nt."

A short time later Guy Wilson was released without charge.

Matthew Webster was charged with Leigh Leigh's murder and sexual assault. It had taken police over three months to press charges against him, even though they had established within ten days that he had lied about his whereabouts, had publicly stated his intention to rape Leigh and had the opportunity to commit the crime.

Matthew Webster was refused bail and remanded in custody both because of the seriousness of the charges and because police feared for his safety if he returned to Stockton.

A few weeks later, Guy Wilson was sentenced for his assault in pushing Leigh to the ground, kicking and spitting on her. He got six months.

A TOWN DIVIDED

Things didn't get any easier for Leigh's family after Matthew's confession. Robyn's house was broken into and when she ran into any of the boys who had been at the party, they swore at her and abused her, even spat on her. The locals described "Fat Matt" as "a gentle giant" who must have been pushed or goaded into what he had done. Most of the town rallied around his family in support. On the other hand, Guy Wilson's family home was badly damaged in what was suspected to be an arson attack, the assumption being that he had ratted on his mate. The town was divided between those who blamed the boys who carried out the rape, degradation and assault of Leigh Leigh and those who blamed the fourteen-year-old girl it had happened to.

Perhaps most chilling of all was the witness statement of one boy who said, "Early in the night as the people were arriving I was talking to [Cory] and he said, 'Are all the baldies coming tonight?' and I said as far as I know they were. The baldies are the younger girls in years 7 and 8 at school, which is Leigh Leigh and her group. From this conversation I got the impression they were going to get them pissed and then they were going to root them. That's what I've heard they normally do."

"Baldies" was a reference to a lack of female pubic hair. This witness was stating that it was common practice for the older boys to choose underage girls who had just started high school to invite to parties for the express purpose of getting them drunk and raping them. This report is even more sinister knowing that there were girls as young as ten at the party.

The names of some of the boys who had surrounded Leigh as she lay in the fetal position on the ground, and followed her when she tried to get away had been passed around the town. The people who blamed the assailants for the crime wanted those boys brought to account, even if they had not played a part in her murder. They were also angry at the knowledge that half the party—both boys and girls—must have witnessed what was happening to Leigh, yet nearly all of them refused to come forward.

However, an equal number put the blame squarely on Leigh for attending the party, getting drunk and having sex on the beach. Even though there was substantial evidence that she had not consented, by that time any suggestion of rape had been dropped from the charges. The charges brought against the three culprits—carnal knowledge, common assault and murder—created the legal fiction that Leigh had not been raped at all. To some townsfolk, that meant she had been a willing participant. Leigh's ordinary late-spring outfit of shorts, tank top and sneakers was suddenly described as "revealing" and inviting trouble. One girl, the same age as Leigh, told ABC's *Background Briefing*, "A lot of people said she was a slut and she deserved it. I remember my mum telling me that."

The kids at the party who were suspected of leaking information to the police about the party were bullied, attacked or ostracized. Police did not seem interested in following up charges against any of the other teenagers in attendance, but they assured Robyn that the truth would come out at the trial of her daughter's killer.

Media attention turned to the lack of parental supervision at the party and the presence of drugs and alcohol. What did they expect, letting hormonal teenagers run wild like that? According to some papers, the parents were as much to blame as the culprit was.

By the time Matthew Webster went to trial, the narrative had changed from a vicious gang rape of an underage girl by several assailants who carried out both sexual and common assault, to an act of unpremeditated violence by a single person, Matthew Webster.

Leigh Leigh's family became increasingly shunned by the Stockton community. Meanwhile, many in the town rallied around Matthew Webster's family, sympathizing at the horrible situation that had befallen them.

The leaking of the atrocities carried out on Leigh that night, along with the unfounded rumors about Leigh's behavior and promiscuity pushed her father into attempting to commit suicide in September 1990. He slashed his wrists at home and would have died if a friend hadn't arrived and found him on the floor, barely conscious and surrounded by a pool of blood. He was rushed to hospital for surgery.

Leigh's stepfather, Brad Shearman, spent a week in a mental hospital because of the stress of his memories, exacerbated by being viewed as a suspect by the towns- folk. He still carried the picture in his mind of the bloody, broken, naked body of his stepdaughter lying in the sand- hills that terrible morning.

The pressure became too much for Robyn Leigh and Brad Shearman, and they separated in September 1990.

THE "GENTLE GIANT"

On October 22, 1990, Matthew Webster pleaded guilty in the Supreme Court of New South Wales to murdering Leigh Leigh. He had admitted to walking with Leigh down to the sandhills where he tried to remove her clothes to have sex with her. When she resisted, he grew angry and grabbed her around the throat, choking her until she passed out. He killed her as an act of impulse because he was scared that she would squeal on him about the attempted sexual assault.

In his own words, Matthew Webster said, "She was punching and pushing and I grabbed her by the throat and she said 'Don't' and I choked her a bit, she stopped punching and I grabbed the rock and I killed her... I thought she would squeal on me for trying to rape her."

After the murder he said he ran to a nearby boat ramp and washed his hands in a sink, then ran home through back streets. Later that night he met up with several of the partygoers back at Roberto's, and told them he left earlier to go for a beer at the Stockton Hotel. He admitted he lied about going to the hotel to give himself an alibi.

Several character witnesses described Matthew as a gentle giant, quiet, emotionally immature and lacking in self-confidence. He had consumed a large amount of alcohol and cannabis that night, which made him act out of character.

A psychologist called to provide insight into Matthew Webster's motivation said that Leigh fighting off his advances was the ultimate rejection. According to this theory, once it became known that Leigh had had sex with Cory on the beach, the other boys all felt entitled to also have sex with her. As far as they were concerned, she had proven herself to be a slut who would have sex with anyone. She deserved to be degraded. The psychologist said, "Webster attacked Leigh Leigh, not so much because she would not let him have sex with her but because she became the living proof that even a slut, the property of the clan, thought he was not good enough to have sex with her. It is for this reason that he proceeded to strangle her. All the pent up rage which Webster had managed to control for most of his life was unleashed, not only by the drugs and alcohol, but by what he perceived to be an extreme rejection."

On October 24, 1990, Justice Wood sentenced Matthew Webster, to twenty years in prison, with a non-parole period of fourteen years.

The judge's sentencing remarks offered little comfort to Leigh Leigh's family. In fact, it seemed to lay some of the blame at their feet. Justice Wood said:

It is entirely reprehensible that this party should have been allowed to take place without adult supervision to prevent the unlawful abuse of alcohol and drugs and the considerable amount of promiscuous sexual activity which took place between a large number of teenagers present... A duty is owed to all young persons to ensure that they are protected from the inevitable peer group pressures at functions such as this, to experiment with and to abuse alcohol and drugs and to engage in sexual promiscuity of the kind which occurred here. Those pressures are exceedingly strong. They cannot be swept under the carpet and it can only be said that the tragic killing of Leigh was totally unnecessary and totally preventable. It should not have been left to the police to check on this party or to endeavor to exercise control over functions such as this. Police have other valuable work to do and the care of young teenagers cannot be delegated to them. It is the responsibility of parents who organize such parties, or who allow their children to attend, to ensure that they are appropriately supervised and that the children are properly counselled about the dangers in the use of alcohol and drugs and also in relation to intimate relationships.

Of the murderer, the judge said:

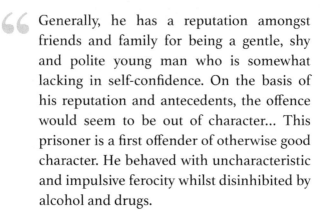

> Generally, he has a reputation amongst friends and family for being a gentle, shy and polite young man who is somewhat lacking in self-confidence. On the basis of his reputation and antecedents, the offence would seem to be out of character... This prisoner is a first offender of otherwise good character. He behaved with uncharacteristic and impulsive ferocity whilst disinhibited by alcohol and drugs.

Perhaps nobody told the judge about Matthew's violent assault a few months earlier of a boy who had teased him.

When he spoke of what Leigh endured, the judge's language suggested that she had not been raped at all, but rather "sexual intercourse took place." His remarks in full were:

> "The victim, Leigh Leigh, was one who became affected by alcohol early in the night. At one stage she went to the sand dunes where sexual intercourse took place with a fifteen-year-old male person. She had previously been a virgin. The fifteen-year-old was later sentenced to community service for his sexual assault upon her.
>
> "Shortly after returning to the club house she spoke of having had sex with this young person and of being pregnant. She was obviously distressed but this led to her being subjected to verbal abuse by a

number of male persons, including the prisoner and Wilson. This abuse extended to her being spat on and having beer poured over her as she lay on the ground. She was also kicked and a bottle was thrown at her at one stage as she tried to stagger away. She went inside the club house where she was again spat on and had beer poured over her by the prisoner and another person.

"She then left the club house and sat on a grassed area a short distance away. The prisoner approached and walked her to a depression in the sand dunes approximately 100 metres away from the club house where he forcibly removed her clothing for the purpose of having sexual intercourse. He placed a finger in her vagina. She resisted and the prisoner then placed his hands around her throat and choked her to the point of rendering her unconscious. He then walked about five feet away and picked up a large piece of rock weighing approximately six kilograms, walked back to where she was lying and threw the rock, striking her twice on the left side of the head. These blows occasioned massive injuries, caving in the left side of her face and head and bringing about instant death."

Outside the court, Matthew Webster's family was combative with the attending media, with his father spitting out, "I hope youse all burn in hell."

VICTIMIZED AGAIN

The diminishing of the sexual assaults on Leigh devastated her family. The initial police reports stated firmly that she had been raped—possibly gang raped. When it came to testifying, the story had been changed that to say there was no evidence of any rape. The damage done to her vaginal area was consistent with violent, repeated, unwanted intrusion, possibly with a beer bottle, but those details were withheld from the court. A coroner's report to police revealed that Leigh had been sexually assaulted more than once before being brutally beaten to death.

Robyn later told ABC's *Background Briefing*, "[Detective] Chaffey admitted he had lied to me when he told me that he had no evidence that Leigh was raped. He said that, yes, Leigh had been gang raped, and yes in his belief [Cory] did rape Leigh but it was [Cory's] word against a dead person. He told me I had no say in whether others should be charged with Leigh's murder or rape. He also told me this was a private conversation which he would deny publicly ever being a party to, so there was no point me mouthing off about it to anyone."

In an academic article produced after the judge's comments were made public, Professor Kerry Carrington, a feminist writer and academic, pointed out how the wording of the judge and how the case was presented had the effect of blaming the victim for the horrific crime that had happened to her. The professor wrote:

 Justice Wood's judgment made no reference whatsoever to the sexual violence which the victim endured prior to her murder. His judgment expressed considerable concern about 'sexual promiscuity' that occurred at the party attended by the victim and her assailants and the 'lack of parental supervision.' Justice Wood's judgment also considerably diminished the extent of collective violence inflicted upon Leigh at the party just prior to her murder, stating, 'Only a small group of men mistreated her.'

Justice Wood described Matthew Webster as 'a first offender of otherwise good character,' who 'behaved with uncharacteristic and impulsive ferocity whilst disinhibited by alcohol and drugs.' By contrast Leigh Leigh was represented in the judge's comments as a victim of a parental failure and as a willing participant in a wild party involving sexual promiscuity and the reckless consumption of drugs and alcohol. We have argued that this reversing of the attribution of guilt and innocence rendered the victim the offender, and her attacker, a victim. Justice Wood's comments on the sentence made ready copy for the press and attracted criticism from the mother of the victim who was forced to publicly defend her own and her daughter's reputations.

The media also picked up on the judge's comments about the unsupervised wild party where promiscuous teenagers drank and took drugs and ran articles to that effect. A lengthy and detailed feature article in the *Good Weekend*, "In Cold Blood," seemed to pile on the victim-blaming. In reporting that the judge had decreed that Cory and Leigh had consensual sex the night of her death, the reporter (who was also the local crime reporter for the *Newcastle Herald*) even implied that Leigh had instigated it, saying "Leigh Leigh had chosen November 3, 1989 as the day to make the move she had assured her mother was at least two years away."

That article painted a picture of a rebellious teenager who had lied to her mother and gone to the party with the intention of getting drunk, taking drugs and having sex. It also seemed to place part of the blame at her mother's feet.

 Robyn maintained an open mother–daughter relationship with Leigh. Probably as a result of that relationship, Leigh developed an outlook on life that was older than her years. They discussed sex often as Leigh moved through puberty. Robyn remembers that her daughter also developed quicker physically than her friends, assuming the body of a woman at age fourteen that made her the subject of admiration among some girlfriends and of acute jealousy among others. It also ensured that she acquired a trail of male admirers.

The reporter quoted a local priest, Father David Denley, who conducted Leigh's funeral, as saying, "You don't see that many kids on the streets at night now, which is a good thing. It is often said that something good often comes from the worst thing, and in this area I suppose it is that parents have begun to question the level of control they exercise over their children. I think Stockton feels that it has been made a scapegoat for Australian society's realization that too much freedom can have disastrous effects."

The reports all talked about permissive parents, unsupervised parties, drugs, alcohol and underage sex. What they didn't talk about was a culture of violence among teenage boys in many parts of rural and urban Australia. In the 1980s, women's liberation and feminism were still in their growth phase and the self-esteem movement that taught teenage girls that they were worth more than their perceived value to boys had not yet reached rural Australia. Often the decision of whether or not sex was going to occur was the boy's alone, and even if a girl resisted she might well be branded a "slut" after the event. Boys and young men blamed the girls or women whom they coveted if they felt undesirable, and that blame manifested itself in behaviors that ranged from "slut-shaming" to violence. Today they are recognized as "incels" but such labels didn't exist in 1980s Stockton.

There was a feeling in the Stockton community that the local police understood that their boys were good kids who might have taken things a bit too far and deserved to be let off the hook. They certainly didn't deserve to have their lives ruined because of one stupid girl. You couldn't stop the fact that "boys will be boys."

Matthew Webster appealed his sentence, but in July 1991, the NSW Court of Appeal upheld the sentence, much to the relief of Leigh's family.

THE OTHER PERPETRATORS

After most of the publicity died down, Robyn Leigh continued to grapple with the knowledge that others had been involved in assaulting her daughter and they had never been charged, nor did it look like they ever would be. She also struggled with the changed narrative from the beginning, when police were confident Leigh had been violently raped, probably by several people, to the description in court that she had had consensual sex with one person and her murderer had merely "inserted his finger into her vagina." Those descriptions in no way explained the severe damage done to Leigh Leigh's genitals, as detailed in the coroner's report.

Some of the details in Matthew Webster's confession didn't match the evidence. The blood spatters showed that the blows to Leigh with a heavy object had come from different directions, indicating more than one person could have been involved. He claimed to have choked Leigh with his left hand, but the postmortem report said the bruises on her neck were consistent with a right hand. Detective Chaffey, who led the investigation, denied he had evidence that Leigh was raped as there was no semen inside her, yet the report described in graphic detail very severe genital injuries consistent with an extremely violent sexual assault.

The evidence and the reports that had not been considered in court led to the conclusion that it was possible that more than one person had killed Leigh Leigh and that Matthew Webster had agreed to take the fall.

By 1992, Robyn Leigh was forced to flee Stockton after an ongoing campaign of harassment. Her home was broken into and people threatened to "do the same" to her and her daughter. To many, Robyn was the embodiment of an incident that had brought shame and unwanted publicity to their town. Stockton wanted to get on with life, and Robyn's presence wasn't helping achieve that goal.

Despite the locals wanting Leigh Leigh's case swept under the rug, there were many people, particularly feminist commentators, who maintained the rage of the mishandling at every step of Leigh's rape and murder. They railed against the blatant and cruel victim-blaming of both Judge Wood's sentencing remarks and the publicity that came on the back of them.

Leading the charge was Professor Kerry Carrington, who had spent years poring over every aspect of Leigh Leigh's case. She wrote that Newcastle culture "seemed to exhibit a high level of tolerance for sexual violence among its adolescent population. I was interested in how this culture overlapped with the local surfing culture, the occupational culture of the BHP steelworks, and the notorious hard-edged working-class culture of the city."

Professor Carrington studied the court records, statements and news articles and interviewed many of the people involved. She wrote several articles detailing the evidence she had found that more than one person had been involved in Leigh's murder and that several people who should have been charged with offences stemming from that night had completely escaped justice. Even if there was only one murderer, she argued that the murder had come at the culmination of an escalation of degradation and violence over the course of the evening. She became a vocal critic of the police handling of the case and an advocate for true justice for Leigh.

In January 1994, Robyn Leigh wrote to Professor Carrington, "I am the mother of Leigh Leigh... For the last four and a half years I have been fighting for the truth of what really happened that night to be told... The way the police handled the whole case sickens me... I have written to anyone I could think who could help me. But all the politicians, police, ombudsman, Commissioner for Human Rights all ignored my pleas for help... I appreciate you writing to [the] paper and standing up for Leigh. People forget Leigh was the victim; not the boys, Stockton or the kids at the party but Leigh... I have a court case coming up soon and am praying to anyone who will listen to the truth on what really happened that night... I thank you from my heart for speaking out on Leigh's behalf."

Professor Carrington later said it was this personal

plea that spurred her deeper involvement and continuing research into the case. She arranged for Academics for Justice to fund Robyn's appeal against her victim's compensation case and introduced her to a lawyer from the Newcastle Legal Centre to act for her. In May 1993, Robyn and Jessie had been awarded a combined total of $29,214 in victim compensation, an amount that was woefully inadequate for the pain and suffering they had endured. Aided by Professor Carrington's research, they lodged an appeal against the original payout.

They also wanted to have Leigh Leigh's case reopened so that there would be an official record that Leigh was raped and others could be brought to justice. Professor Carrington arranged for a number of fresh forensic opinions to be sought on the autopsy report and other materials. One of these experts, Dr Ruth Armstrong, said in her affidavit, "As a female general practitioner, I examine normal and abnormal female genitalia on a daily basis. The injuries described to Leigh Leigh's genitals are consistent with non-consensual intercourse of an extremely violent nature."

Another expert, Professor Harry Boettcher, concluded that the blows to Leigh's head came from different directions and also theorized that someone may have been restraining her as Matthew Webster hit her.

Professor Carrington's findings specifically pointed to the deeper involvement of two boys, of whom she wrote, "On the basis of our knowledge about this case, we believe there is considerable evidence to support reopening a prosecutorial investigation against two boys who both had a motive to kill Leigh, both being involved in previous assaults upon her (one of which was the sexual assault Leigh complained about), and neither of whom had reliable alibis for the time of the murder. An eyewitness to the last of the three assaults on Leigh provides crucial incriminating evidence connecting these two boys with Webster's movements to the timing of the murder which we believe occurred between 10.15 and 10.30 p.m. This statement was not tendered as an exhibit in Webster's murder trial and is corroborated by another eyewitness statement in our possession and which the investigating police also had at the time."

In an affidavit, the Deputy Director of the NSW Institute of Forensic Medicine had written, "I am of the opinion that it is much more probable that an inflexible object such as a beer bottle, as distinct from a flexible object such as a finger or penis, caused the majority of the genital injuries."

Professor Carrington had a theory on that. In one article she wrote that shortly before her murder, a person she called "Mr. X" "put his arm around her and asked her for a 'root'. Leigh screamed 'No.' She was murdered within the next fifteen minutes. We have been told it was during this time that she sustained most of the injuries to her genital organs as the result of a beer bottle being thrust inside her. We have reason to suspect that this was her 'punishment' for refusing the 'invitation' to 'root'."

In May 1995, in what was described as a landmark legal decision, Judge Joseph Moore approved the appeal from the decision of the Victim's Compensation Tribunal, awarding Leigh's mother and sister an additional $134,048, for a total of $150,000 in compensation.

More importantly, the findings of Judge Moore supported concerns that more than one person may have

been involved in the murder. He concluded, based on a
mountain of evidence, that Leigh was subject to a
number of criminal assaults in the hours before her
murder on November 3, 1989. The first was a rape by a
boy aged fifteen years, charged only with carnal knowledge. The second act of violence involved a number of
boys who spat, kicked, and verbally abused Leigh on the
ground outside and then inside the club house.
According to an article by Jonathan Morrow and Mehera
San Roque, *In Her Death She Remains as the Limit of the
System*, the judgment named six boys involved in the
assaults (whom that article also named). Justice Moore
pointed out that, "One of the assailants, and only one, has
been detected and charged with assault."

The third act of violence was described as an act of
sexual assault "related to the act of murder," "by persons
who have not yet been detected." Justice Moore's
comments also supported Leigh's family's argument that
compelling witness and forensic evidence of sexual
violence had been edited out of the police construction of
the case. Judge Moore said forensic evidence of Leigh's
genital region showed there had been "a severe, violent
and resistant invasion of her body which was performed
by persons who have not been detected."

The findings of Judge Moore, along with the research
by Professor Carrington and other academics, formed the
backbone of a report by the Newcastle Legal Centre to the
NSW Attorney General to have Leigh Leigh's death re-
investigated. On July 26, 1995, the Attorney General urged
the NSW Minister for Police to reopen the investigation
in light of the findings made by Judge Moore.

The report presented to the police minister, Paul

Whelan, by Robyn Leigh's lawyer was hundreds of pages long, with supporting evidence for the allegations that:

(a) there was convincing evidence that more than one person was involved in Leigh's murder;

(b) a range of other assaults were committed against Leigh by more than ten other people who were not prosecuted;

(c) no action was taken by police against young men who admitted sexually assaulting other young women; and

(d) assaults against other people went undetected.

Acknowledging that nobody had ever been charged with Leigh's sexual assault, the police minister stated the upcoming review was "our one opportunity to right the terrible wrongs that occurred on the night that Leigh died." In his statement to Parliament on October 15, 1996, Paul Whelan said, "The New South Wales Crime Commission has the powers needed to get this job done, but it is time for those who know what happened to come forward; it is time to stop the lies and cover-ups and to set the record straight; it is time for the truth to out."

CRIME COMMISSION INQUIRY

W hen word got out that she was trying to have Leigh's case reopened and more boys charged, Robyn Leigh was forced to flee her home after receiving death threats from people who wanted the case left alone. The community of Stockton just wanted it all to go away. They did not want to hear that any of their other sons might have been involved in this murder that had become a blight on the town.

One local woman said to ABC's *Background Briefing*, "I think that there was more involved. But I don't know whether it's too late to bring it up now. I mean most people have got on with their lives. It's been seven years. And it's a sad thing for Matthew Webster's family for it all to be brought up again. And I think it's just been left too late really."

Matthew Webster talked to the media about the murder for the first time in 1996, and insisted that he acted alone in killing Leigh and was not covering for anyone.

Professor Carrington released a book, *Who Killed Leigh Leigh: a story of shame and mateship in an Australian town*, which criticized police over their handling of the investigation and laid out the evidence she had amassed about the events that happened that night.

The Crime Commission hearing offered another blow to the family of Leigh Leigh when it released its findings on March 31, 1998. The Commission found that the crime occurred exactly as described in court during the sentencing hearings; that Matthew Webster alone was responsible for Leigh's death; that while some of the police investigation methods were inappropriate, they did not lead to important relevant facts being omitted for the purpose of sentence proceedings; and that while not disagreeing that the evidence suggested that other persons could have been charged with offences committed on the night of the murder, police did not act inappropriately in failing to do so. There would be no further action taken in relation to Leigh Leigh's murder.

The commission did, however, make adverse findings against some police involved in the case, and referred the matter to the Police Integrity Commission to determine whether the police involved had acted properly. These, however, were in relation to the unlawful arrests of Matthew Webster and fifteen-year-old Cory.

Robyn Leigh was exhausted. She had spent nearly ten years trying to get justice for her daughter. She finally decided to give up. It was clear that Stockton was always going to protect its sons and would never help her get justice.

POLICE INTEGRITY COMMISSION
INQUIRY

The police officers involved were all called to give evidence in the Police Integrity Commission investigation, as was Professor Carrington, though she was not informed why. She was cross-examined more thoroughly, more aggressively and for longer than any other witness. Other academic observers of the case believed that she had been set up and was summoned "for the sole purpose of attacking her credibility on issues they had no intention of investigating, and to discredit someone who had attracted considerable media attention for criticizing police."

During cross-examination, Professor Carrington maintained that she believed that it was a "common purpose" murder and that other persons were involved in a criminological sense, but it was now her belief that Matthew Webster had acted alone, in a legal sense, when he murdered Leigh Leigh. She said, "On closer examination of the material, I didn't come to that conclusion, and —but I've sat through six days of hearings here. I've read the Crime Commission report and my views have changed."

The Commission's review was released in October 2000. When Robyn Leigh attended Newcastle Legal Centre to meet with members of the Police Integrity Commission, she still held on to a glimmer of hope that they would tell her that the investigation into Leigh's death had been reopened and the other culprits would be hunted down and punished.

Instead, she was told that the commission had found the police had acted properly in relation to the investigation and confirmed that nobody else would be charged. However, as a final insult, they told her that the findings of the commission could offer Matthew Webster a possible avenue for appeal. There was evidence that he had been detained unlawfully when he was picked up by police before he confessed, and quite likely had been assaulted by police at that time. In addition, Cory had not been provided an opportunity to contact his parents when he was arrested, despite being only fifteen. The review had recommended the dismissal of Detective Sergeant Chaffey for gross dereliction in duty in relation to the arrests.

In an attempt to make Robyn feel better, the police painstakingly went through photos of every person who had been confirmed as having been at the party and told her what had become of them in the decade since. None of them had amounted to much: some were in prison, others were drug addicts and most of the girls were single mothers or in domestic violence situations.

Hearing about their crappy lives did not help Robyn at all. It didn't bring any justice to Leigh.

JUSTICE DENIED

The potential avenue for appeal apparently didn't go anywhere and Matthew Webster served out his sentence. In 2003, in preparation for his imminent release, he started a program of day and weekend leave from prison. By all accounts, Matthew's time in prison wasn't too difficult. He was popular among other inmates and spent time in the gym working out. A few months before he was due for his parole hearing, he began work release, reporting back to the prison at the end of each day. His employer reported he was performing well and that they intended to keep him in that position.

Matthew Webster was granted parole in June 2004, having served fourteen years of his twenty-year sentence for one of the most heinous crimes in Australia's history. The NSW Parole Board stipulated that he not live in Stockton, or the larger Newcastle area, for at least the next six years, meaning he would not be able to go to live back at his mother's house. Instead he was to move into a halfway house in Sydney.

A news report at the time quoted his family as being pleased. "Relatives of murderer Matthew Grant Webster are relieved his crime has finally been forgiven. Now they would like it to be forgotten," the piece said.

Robyn Leigh stated for the press that she had forgiven Matthew Webster and sympathized with his family. Her best friend publicly wondered whether that was a mother's last desperate attempt to extract from her killer the truth about what happened to her daughter that night. If it was, it didn't work.

Just three months after his release, the "gentle giant" had his parole revoked when he was charged with two counts of assault and maliciously inflicting grievous bodily harm. He had allegedly got into a fight with his girlfriend's former partner. (Matthew's girlfriend had also previously been charged with murder but was acquitted. It was found to be a case of self-defense as she believed the person was threatening to harm her unborn baby.) The victim suffered a broken jaw and cracked ribs as a result of the alleged altercation. The man also claimed that Matthew Webster had pulled a knife on him. The charges were eventually dropped due to lack of evidence and Matthew was released again later that year.

The case of Leigh Leigh has been the subject of many academic articles and is taught in law schools in Australia as an extreme example of victim-blaming, both in the courtroom and in the media. The boys who gathered around Leigh that night, abusing and assaulting her with such callousness are adults now. They may even have daughters of their own and warn them that somewhere out there are boys and men just like them waiting for their little girl to come along. Men who would hit, kick and spit upon a distressed schoolgirl, rather than coming to her aid. Many still live by the creed that it is "un-Australian" to dob in a mate. Nobody thought to mention it was un-Australian to beat, rape, spit on and humiliate a fourteen-year-old child

Leigh's case became the basis of a play, *The Property of the Clan*, later renamed *Blackrock*, which was a fictionalized account concentrating on the aftermath and fallout of rape and murder at a teenage party. The play was performed in schools, although Newcastle High School declined to allow it to be performed there. When the play toured regional Australia, one of the frightening observations the playwright made was that, in more than one town, locals thought the events were a fictionalized account of incidents that had happened in *their* towns—similar group rapes that had ended in the death of a girl in one case, and a victim being left for dead (although she survived) in another. The chilling conclusion was that what happened to Leigh Leigh before her murder was not uncommon in those towns. Many times the victims themselves were complicit in the cover-up of their own assaults for fear of being revictimized in the form of "slut-shaming," just as had happened to Leigh.

Blackrock was also later made into a movie, where much of the vile, misogynist language of the play was toned down. There is another major difference in the film version. Jared, a character who witnessed the vicious rape, breaks the code of silence, refusing to provide the killer with an alibi, and the murderer commits suicide rather than get arrested. Jared is an entirely fictional construct, though the character has been interpreted as a metaphor for everyone who witnessed Leigh being publicly assaulted yet did nothing.

As Professor Carrington put it, "The brutal rape and murder of Leigh Leigh which followed hours of brutalization by a group of Stockton boys is one of the most heinous crimes in recent Australian legal history. Yet most of the boys involved in this extremely brutal crime have escaped prosecution completely and continue to be protected from prosecution. Nowhere has the public interest in securing justice for Leigh Leigh been represented in this criminal investigation."

For Leigh Leigh, that code of silence was never broken and her family has lost all hope that justice will ever truly be served.

PART IV

MARTHA PUEBLA (AGE 16)

VINELAND BOYZ GO CRUISING

On November 23, 2002, three members of Los Angeles gang the Vineland Boyz were cruising in their Mustang convertible on the way back from a birthday celebration at the gravesite of "Clever," one of their fallen comrades.

The Vineland Boyz gang was an offshoot of the notorious 18th Street Gang, one of the largest criminal gangs in LA, which boasted up to 50,000 members across the U.S as well as an alliance with the Mexican Mafia. In the early 1980s, a rebellious group broke away from the 18th Street Gang and formed a new club, calling themselves the Vineland Boyz after Vineland Street in North Hollywood, where some of the crew played football. The 18th Street Gang considered the formation of this new gang by its own members to be a betrayal, and the tensions turned into a war between the two gangs, which lasted decades and cost members of both sides their lives.

Street gangs in Los Angeles during the 1980s and 1990s were expected to comply with traditional gang conduct and regulations laid down and enforced by the Mexican Mafia. Following several events that the Mexican Mafia considered transgressions of their code, they announced the Vineland Boyz were fair game, and the founder of the Vineland Boyz was murdered by a rival gang. As the new century rolled around, the Vineyard Boyz tried to smooth things over with the Mexican Mafia. In their attempts to ingratiate themselves back into the fold, they built up a reputation of extreme violence and recklessness. Their members were considered some of the hardest men around, willing to use violence at the slightest provocation and to establish control.

Unlike most gangs, the Vineland Boyz didn't wear gang uniforms or colors, preferring to dress smartly and give off the air of businessmen. By 2002, the Vineland Boyz, comprised mainly of Hispanic Americans who controlled much of the San Fernando Valley drug trade, had gained widespread notoriety. They engaged in, among other things, murder, narcotics trafficking, money laundering, racketeering and intimidation of witnesses.

Full of booze, drugs and testosterone that November night, when the three young gang members came across twenty-six-year-old Enrique Acosta sitting in his car on Lankershim Boulevard in North Hollywood, they decided to confront him. Suspicious of any stranger, they demanded to know where he was from. When Enrique responded, "Canoga Park," which was the territory of a rival gang, one of the men responded by shooting him in the head and body, killing him.

Four days later, shortly before 2 a.m. on November 27, 2002, sixteen-year-old Martha Puebla was lying in bed in her home at 11057 Lull Street, Sun Valley in California, when she heard a tap at her ground-floor window. Peering out, she recognized a close friend. Looking down the path, she could just make out a car parked on the street beyond the tall white wall, right outside her front gate.

Martha opened the window and her friend tried to convince her to sneak out to hang out with her and her boyfriend, eighteen-year-old Christian Vargas, who was waiting in the car. Such antics were commonplace for the teens, who had grown up in tough, gang-dominated Los Angeles neighborhoods. The girls were no angels, and Martha had a loose allegiance to the Vineland Boyz, having dated at least one of their members.

As the girls chatted, and Martha debated whether to head out into the early hours of the morning, a lone man in a hooded sweatshirt approached the car where Christian Vargas waited. Gunshots rang out into the night, causing Martha's friend to jump through the window. The two girls cowered in Martha's room, until they got up the nerve to peek over the windowsill at the car sitting in the darkness.

When they were sure the hooded man had gone, the girls gingerly approached the car. Christian Vargas' body was riddled with bullets, but he was still alive. He begged the girls for help, but before it could come, he slumped forward against the steering wheel and died.

AN ARREST

The police soon swarmed the street. They separated the two girls, who appeared to be the only witnesses to the slaying. Among the police officers were homicide detective Martin Pinner and his partner Juan Rodriguez. When they questioned Martha's friend, she claimed that Martha had cried out, "It was Peps!" as soon as they heard the shots. Peps was the nickname of Jose Ledesma, one of the Vineland Boyz, and Martha's ex-boyfriend.

Martha, however, vigorously denied the claim. She said she had not seen the gunman, and only speculated with her friend if the assailant was one of the Vineland Boyz as they sheltered beneath the windowsill. The sixteen-year-old was tough—she knew the way of the streets and she had no intention of telling the cops anything.

With the reputation of the gang well-known in the area, it was little wonder that Martha Puebla remained tight-lipped around police officers. She was both loyal to the Vineland Boyz and afraid of them. She trusted the gang, but she knew that anyone who snitched would have a target on them.

Despite Martha clamming up, Martin Pinner and Juan Rodriguez were very familiar with the Vineland Boyz and felt the lead of Jose Ledesma was a strong one. Nineteen-year-old Jose was already wanted for questioning in connection with the murder of Enrique Acosta, just four days earlier. Ballistic testing on the shell casings from the crime scenes of Christian Vargas and Enrique Acosta determined they were fired from the same 9mm semiautomatic handgun. Given that Jose was already a suspect in one murder and his name had come up in the second murder, the detectives were confident that he was their man.

Obtaining a search warrant for Jose's home was a simple matter, and the two detectives went through it that night. Their search turned up a loaded assault rifle hidden beneath Jose's mattress and letters from other Vineland Boyz who had been incarcerated. However, Jose wasn't there, and the detectives were told that he was out with another Vineland Boyz member, twenty-four-year-old Mario Catalan, also suspected of being one of the men involved in Enrique's murder. However, nobody was willing or able to say exactly where the two gang members were.

Word soon got to Jose that the police had been through his house. Instead of returning home, Jose Ledesma and Mario Catalan fled across the border, joined by Mario's girlfriend, and the three disappeared into Mexico.

It's quite likely that would have been the end of it, and

the murders chalked up to just another couple of unsolved gangland slayings, except that two days later Mexican police were called to attend a domestic violence situation at a Tijuana motel. There they found Jose, Mario and Mario's girlfriend blind drunk after a day of heavy drinking at a seaside resort. Mario was in the midst of assaulting his girlfriend, who quickly told the police that her lover and his friend were wanted over the murder in Lankershim Boulevard.

That very night, Jose and Mario were hauled back into Los Angeles. Detectives recovered a 9mm semiautomatic handgun from the green Altima driven by Mario when they fled to Mexico. They found about $3,200 in cash on Mario, which they believed he planned to use to bribe Mexican jail officials to protect him from U.S. authorities seeking his extradition on the murder charge.

Without being given time to sleep, the young men were taken to separate interview rooms where they were read their Miranda rights.

Detectives Pinner and Rodriguez interviewed Jose. He didn't request a lawyer and flatly denied any involvement in the two murders. He insisted they had arrested the wrong person and that he would be able to provide an alibi for that night.

The detectives tried all their usual methods, but Los Angeles gangbangers are notoriously hard to crack, especially teenagers who have something to prove to the mob. Prison for Jose was just another rite of passage and he laughed and swore at the detectives, showing no signs of fear, remorse or inclinations to confess.

Detectives in the U.S. are under no obligation to tell the truth when interrogating suspects. They are allowed to lie to elicit a confession. The most common lies that they tell are about physical evidence, such as claiming to have fingerprints or DNA from the scene of the crime that matches the suspect. They can lie about having eyewitnesses and the confessions of accomplices.

Detective Pinner told Jose that the police had evidence to prove he was the lone gunman who shot Christian Vargas. "I have multiple witnesses who are going to testify that you were the shooter," he said. He then went on to say that he knew Jose had been on his way to Martha Puebla's house to visit her that night and that they had interviewed Martha straight after the murder.

When Jose still continued to deny both being the shooter and knowing anyone called Martha, Detective Pinner left the room. When he came back, he was brandishing a "six pack," slang for a photographic version of a police lineup used to help witnesses identify a suspect. Jose's picture was circled and beneath it scrawled a handwritten note, which said, "This is who shot my friend's boyfriend." The photo lineup was signed by Martha Puebla.

Jose's feature's tightened, but he maintained his denials, steadfastly admitting to nothing. Detective Rodriguez brought in a photograph of the curvy peroxide-blonde teenager and shoved it in Jose's face. Jose insisted he didn't recognize her.

It appeared the ruse hadn't worked. Detective Pinner played his final card, telling Jose that they had recovered the handgun and it was just a matter of time before forensics matched it to the casings found at the murder scenes.

Other detectives working the Acosta case had had no

better luck with the older and more seasoned Mario, so they finally gave up and put the two men in a holding cell together. Then the detectives retreated, hoping that the two would have incriminating conversations that would be picked up on the bugs they had placed in the cell.

The pair discussed the gun and detectives noted that Jose seemed to be increasingly agitated. Police listened to the recording, but the men did not incriminate themselves for murder.

The next afternoon, Jose was allowed out of the cell to make a phone call. All phone calls from the prison are recorded, and if the detectives had listened to the recording of this one, they would have heard Jose speaking down the line in a mix of Spanish and English to one of his gang mates called Cokester. If the detectives had listened to that tape they would have heard Jose say, "Do you know the slut that lives there by my house? Her name starts with an M. I need her to disappear. She is dropping dimes. But keep a low profile. Stay on your toes, homie. And don't get caught."

MARTHA TESTIFIES

Meanwhile, nobody told Martha about the fictional role she had played in Jose's case. Far from identifying Jose out of a lineup, Martha had clammed up, refusing to provide any information at all. Detectives Pinner and Rodriguez had forged her signature on the photograph. She was told that she would be compelled to testify at Jose's preliminary hearing, and the court records noted that she appeared as a reluctant witness.

In the lead up to the hearing, Martha got wind of rumors that Jose and Mario were blaming her for putting Jose at the scene of Christian Vargas' murder outside her house. Martha assumed this was because of what her friend had told police that night. She allegedly threatened her girlfriend, telling her that if she cooperated with authorities Martha would tell the Vineland Boyz where the girl's family lived.

The preliminary hearing for the slaying of both Jose and Mario came to court on May 1, 2003. Martha was forced to testify, but she was a most unhelpful witness, repeating what she had told the detectives on the morning of the shooting. The prosecutors asked her to point to the shooter in court and she claimed she could not do so. She had not seen the shooter before, during or after the event. She had simply heard shots fired and had not seen anything at all.

A few members of the public had come along to the hearing, including Juan Catalan, Mario's brother. He'd had to provide his license as identification upon entering the courthouse. Juan listened to the teenager's testimony and then he left.

"YOU KNOW ME"

A bit over a week later, at around 10.00 p.m. on May 12, 2003, Martha Puebla was sitting on the curb outside her house. She wore a white sweater that hugged her figure, blue jeans and blue-and-white Nike sneakers, pulled on casually with the laces left loose. The house was on a large corner block and when Martha was out on the curb she was far enough away that her mother couldn't hear her conversation from inside.

That warm spring evening she had been chatting to friend. None of them really noticed the four-door 2000 Chevy Malibu with tinted windows that circled the block a few times. As the night wore on, only one friend remained on the curb to keep Martha company. She barely noticed the man who approached from behind just after 10.30 p.m.. He came from the Case Street side of the house where the car that had been circling was idling, with somebody still at the wheel. He walked straight up to Martha and demanded, "Who are you?"

She replied, "I'm Martha. You know me."

The man didn't hesitate. He reached into his pocket and pulled out a 9mm handgun—the same kind of gun used to slaughter Christian Vargas in almost that same spot six months earlier. He fired several shots, but there was really no need. He was so close that the first, fatal shot beneath Martha's left eye left residue and burn marks on her cheek.

Martha went down instantly, falling backwards on the curb toward the sidewalk, where she lay with her eyes open but unseeing, staring at the night sky. Hearing the shots, neighbors poked their heads out; the braver ones came outside out and took note of the man who was running away from the scene, gun still in his hand. Martha's mother was one who ventured out. When she saw her daughter, she let out a scream that could be heard around the neighborhood. Her words were in Spanish, but her anguish was clear. She was screaming, "My God! She's dead!"

For the second time in six months, police swarmed the area and did what they needed to do to preserve the crime scene. Police tape was put up, photographs were taken, and evidence was tagged and bagged.

As usual, if there was anybody in the area who saw the assailant, they were prudently keeping the information to themselves. Neighbors knew that Martha ran with gang members and nobody wanted to be involved in something like that. They told the police they had seen a suspicious car circling the block but were light on detail.

Officers comforted Martha's parents, who had been just feet away when their daughter was gunned down.

When they heard Martha's name, something clicked in the mind of the police supervisor at the scene. He put in a call to detective Martin Pinner to let him know that one of his homicide witnesses was dead.

A SUSPECT

Detectives Pinner and Rodriguez knew that Martha must have been murdered either as retaliation for testifying against Jose Ledesma at the preliminary hearing, or to ensure she would not be able to testify against him at trial. Her murder also served as a powerful warning to any other potential witnesses to think twice about cooperating with law enforcement and testifying at future criminal proceedings related to the Vineland Boyz.

Martha's friend had fled when she was shot. In his rush to get away, he dropped his cell phone and police used that to track him down. They were immediately suspicious of him and grilled him as though he was a suspect. He insisted he was not the gunman, and was reluctant to become further involved, but assisted them in putting together an identikit. He described the suspect who fled the scene as a medium-built male Hispanic, nineteen to twenty-five years of age, 5'8" to 5'10". He had very short hair and a moustache and appeared to be a gang member. An artist drew a composite sketch of the man police should be looking for.

Martha's parents, Martha Rauda and Regulo Puebla, who did not speak English, were moved interstate by the City of Los Angeles for their own protection. Nobody from the city or the police department told them that detectives Pinner and Rodriguez had falsely advised Jose Ledesma that Martha had identified him and circled his picture in the six pack.

On June 7, 2003, the Los Angeles City Council offered a $25,000 reward for information leading to the arrest and conviction of the person responsible for the murder of Martha Puebla.

They continued sifting through the witness statements and matching them up with known associates of the gang members. The problem was, the description of the assailant matched any number of the gang members, as did the composite sketch. Young, dark-haired Latinos sporting a moustache were not exactly in short supply in the area.

Eventually they settled on someone who they considered matched the description. He lived five blocks from Martha. What's more, he was the brother of Mario Catalan and he had been in court the day that Martha testified. The detectives pulled up a mugshot they had on file of Juan Catalan and made a six pack of Juan alongside other men of similar appearance. Detectives Pinner and Rodriguez took this to their witnesses to see if anyone could positively identify him.

JUAN CATALAN

J uan Catalan was born in Los Angeles, California, in 1978 and grew up in the suburbs of Sun Valley, 18 miles north of the city. From the time he could walk, his major passion was sports. He had dreamt of growing up to be a basketball player and followed the Lakers religiously. When it came to American football, he was a 49ers fan. With baseball, he followed the footsteps of his family and rooted for the Dodgers.

Juan grew up going to baseball games with his father and uncle. Some of his earliest memories were of going to see the games in the very cheapest seats, known as the "nosebleed seats" because people joked they were so far away you could get a nosebleed from the thin air at that altitude. Juan and his brother and cousins sat in a row, passing their one pair of binoculars to each other along the line, each kid having an allotted amount of time to watch the action. As a child, Juan always prayed that one day, he would be in the right place at the right time to catch a ball. His prayers were finally answered when he was eighteen, when a player he described as "a Joe Schmo from the Dodger bench" hit a two-run homer in the ninth innings. The ball sailed into the left-field pavilion where Juan was ready, and he took a flawless catch.

There were few highlights like this in Juan's life, which was typical of a Hispanic family doing it rough. His hopes of becoming a professional basketball player were dashed by his practical parents, who expected Juan to go into the family business and work hard like his father did. They had little imagination or time for big dreams, and Juan dropped out of high school and fulfilled their modest expectations.

Juan always looked up to his older brother, Mario. When Mario started hanging around with the wrong crowd as a teenager, he came home with stereos and all types of different car parts. All the cool, free gadgets intrigued Juan, and he agreed to be the driver when Mario and his friends broke into cars. This led eventually to Juan's arrest.

Jail frightened him, and Juan was determined that it would be the first and last time he ever went to prison. As Mario got older, he joined local notorious gang, the Vineland Boyz. Juan didn't follow in his footsteps. Instead, he decided it was more important to keep clean, find a nice girl and settle down for a "family and a white picket fence" kind of life. He met a girl called Alma Oseguera and, by the time he was twenty, the couple had two daughters. Juan worked with his father at the machinery store. It was a tough working-class slog, but one that Juan had been born into and he accepted it as his station in life.

Not all of Juan's family worked blue-collar jobs. One of his cousins worked as a filing clerk for a law firm. When he hung out with Juan, he raved on about how wonderful one of the defense attorneys he worked with was. He told Juan if he ever got into trouble, this guy would be the one to call. Juan listened with one ear, before rolling his eyes and saying to his cousin, "Bro, nobody here needs a lawyer."

Meanwhile, his big brother Mario continued going off the rails, running with the Vineland Boyz, which could mean nothing but trouble. In 2003, the Catalan family was shocked, but not completely surprised to discover Mario had been arrested and charged with a gangland murder. Juan still loved his brother, and he and Alma went along to the court hearings to show Mario that, no matter what he got caught up in, he still had the love and support of his little brother.

Juan's relationship with Alma had its ups and downs and the couple had their fair share of fights. By the time their daughters were four and six, Juan and Alma were living apart, but were still in touch. Neither of them was willing to completely give up on their relationship and both of them were committed to their daughters.

The one thing that stayed constant with Juan was his love of sports. He attended every Dodger, Lakers and 49ers game he could get to. Usually, he was still relegated to the nosebleed section of the stadium, but occasionally he would be lucky enough to get good seats.

Not having any sons, Juan was keen to get his daugh-ters excited about coming to games with him. Six-year-old Melissa didn't really understand what was going on at the games, but she loved the atmosphere. One day in May 2003, Juan was lucky enough to be given four last-minute tickets by a customer of his father's business to a game at Dodger Stadium. The Dodgers were playing the Atlanta Braves. Juan had custody of Melissa that night, so he took her, along with his cousin and another friend who was able to come on short notice.

They were great seats, and it was an exciting game, with a tie going into the ninth innings. When Melissa wanted to go to the bathroom and get something to eat, Juan ushered her out to get some ice-cream. By the time they headed back to their seats, Juan was surprised to find TV cameras blocking their path. A camera operator asked Juan if he minded waiting a few minutes while he got his shot. Juan could still see the pitch from behind the camera, so he politely agreed, though he was keen to get back to the seats.

Eventually the production assistant took pity on Juan and Melissa and waved them through. Juan vaguely registered some balding white guy coming up the stairs and yelling, but he was focused on getting back to his buddies.

It was a disappointing result. The game went from a 4–4 tie to the Atlanta Braves winning 11–4. It was just another game to chalk up with the hundreds Juan had been to before.

"THE PICTURES DON'T LIE"

O n the morning of August 12, 2003, Juan was feeling pretty pleased with himself. He had turned on the charm the night before and convinced Alma to come over and spend the night. Now Alma was dropping Juan off to work in the San Fernando Valley, and their younger daughter was in the back seat, happy that mommy and daddy seemed to be getting along.

It was barely past 6 a.m. when they pulled into the parking lot, but as usual, Juan's father was already at the shop. He prided himself on always being first to work. Alma stopped to let Juan out, when out of nowhere, three vehicles rolled in and parked crossways in front of them, cutting off the car. Confused, Juan opened the passenger door and was immediately face-to-face with a man who had a gun pointed straight at his head.

The gunman wasn't wearing a uniform. Juan thought it must be some sort of holdup, and he was surely dead. But before he knew it, ten undercover police officers swarmed around him, screaming at him to get on his knees. When Juan complied, at least two of the officers violently pinned him to the ground, as they placed him under arrest. Alma and their four-year-old daughter looked on in horror.

The police took Juan to a North Hollywood police station, where he was put in a cell for hours, with nobody telling him why he was there. Eventually, he was brought to an interview room where detectives Pinner and Rodriguez waited to grill him. Juan was still at a loss about why he was there. He said, "You guys got me scared, dude. What's going on?"

The detectives insisted that Juan knew exactly why he was there, and he was equally adamant that he had no idea. "You have the right to remain silent, you understand that?" they asked him.

Juan was mystified. He asked the cops, "I'm under arrest now?"

Six hours after his apprehension, when it appeared that Juan had no intention of cracking, they told him that he had been arrested for murder.

Juan was bewildered. Who did they think he had murdered?

The detectives continued to shoot questions at him. Where was he on the night of May 12? Juan couldn't remember where he was three days ago, let alone three months ago. He told them he had no idea. The police didn't believe him.

Juan pleaded with them, saying, "Please do not do this to me. Please, I'm begging you." He said, "What can I do? Can I take a lie detector test or something?" The police said no.

They told him they had witnesses who said it was Juan who had murdered Martha Puebla that night. They knew his brother had been arrested and they knew Juan had been in court when Martha testified. The detectives showed Juan the six pack that contained his picture, which had been circled with some words scrawled underneath it. It was written in Spanish, but translated to, "This is the guy who I saw doing the shooting." There was a signature beneath it.

Rodriguez snapped at Juan, "You see, the pictures don't lie."

To Juan it all seemed like a bad dream. He continued to beg and plead and protest his innocence, but the police told him to prepare for prison. He insisted that they had made a mistake and cried, "You think you're going to put somebody innocent in jail for something they didn't even do?"

Juan was taken before a county court judge, where the next piece of information he was given was the ultimate nightmare. They would be seeking the death penalty. He was sent for processing at Supermax, the high security prison for the most hardened of criminals, where he went through the humiliation of being crammed naked with 100 other prisoners in a room designed to hold fifty, with every crevice prodded and explored before he was issued his prison uniform.

The file for the murder of Martha Puebla was taken on by Beth Silverman, a tough and smart prosecutor who was proud of her record of never losing a murder conviction. Not one. They called her "The Sniper" because she always sought the death penalty, and much of the time she got it.

JUAN HAS NO ALIBI

As Juan sat in prison, stunned at this turn of events, he recalled his cousin telling him about the hotshot lawyer who worked at the firm where he was a filing clerk. Juan got a message to his cousin asking him to get the lawyer to visit him.

The lawyer was Todd Melnik. Todd was a criminal defense attorney who prided himself on going the extra mile for his clients and sought out cases that required in-depth investigation and analysis. He was young, hungry and hardworking, available to his clients 24/7. He claimed to be able to out-investigate seasoned LAPD detectives through sheer hard work, diligent fact finding and thorough investigations using all the processes and techniques 21st century technology provided to him.

Softly spoken, he had a reputation of being open, kind and humble. One happy client said, "In a town of charlatans, this guy is the real deal."

Todd agreed to visit Juan in prison, though he didn't

immediately promise to take on the case. As he sat and listened to Juan, his eyes widened. He was sure that Juan was innocent. He later told *60 Minutes*, "I could tell by his demeanor. I could tell by his voice. He was an easy read."

He said to Juan, "I'm gonna get you out of here." For the first time, Juan had a glimmer of hope. However, Todd said it was essential that Juan rack his brains, ask his friends, ask Alma, do anything possible to try and remember where he was the night of the murder. The prosecution had a witness, which meant the defense needed an airtight alibi.

Juan went through the darkest days of his life as he desperately tried to recall any details that could help his case. Without an alibi to refute the evidence the detectives had on him, his future was looking very bleak. Juan wondered what he had done to deserve this.

Having grown up knowing the streets, Juan was able to make friends in prison, but what they were telling him didn't fill him with much confidence. When they heard that he was being prosecuted by "The Sniper," they regaled him with tales of other prisoners she had prosecuted who had received at least life sentences, if not the lethal injection that she was pursuing for Juan. His dorm was overcrowded and he was relegated to a thin mattress on the hard, concrete ground. The conditions were disgusting, and there was no respite in the showers, where the drains were backed up and prisoners bathed in their own filth.

He had the support of his family, though he didn't want his daughters seeing him in prison. When he spoke to his little girls, they begged to know when he was coming home. Juan tried his best to keep his conversations with them light and positive, but his heart broke every time they asked when they would see him again. His mother visited and did her best to comfort him. A religious woman, she told him that God would not allow him to be convicted of a crime that he did not commit. She was sure that justice would prevail.

Juan's lawyer told him that, even though the evidence was thin, the six pack where his face was circled and the identification of him scrawled on it by a witness would likely be enough to convict him. He told Juan he needed an alibi, or he would be facing the death penalty.

When Juan wasn't in prison, he was at one of his many hearings held in the courthouse. Most of the time he didn't understand what was going on. He sat uncomfortably shackled to his chair as lawyers spoke for fifteen minutes and then he was returned to his cell, none the wiser as to what was happening.

One time was worse than most. Todd had greeted him at the door, his facial features twisted with concern. He told Juan that it was important that, when he walked into court, he look straight ahead and not look around. Martha's entire family was there. Juan shuffled in with his head down, was handcuffed to the chair as usual and obediently looked straight ahead, but he could see the family in his peripheral vision. Worse, could hear them all sobbing.

As he was being led out the door, Martha's mother screamed in Spanish, "I will never forgive you for what you did to my daughter." Juan felt like somebody had grabbed a dagger and stuck it right in his heart. He could see the anguish in her face and understand her pain, but it killed him that her anger was directed at him.

As he languished in prison, Juan racked his brain, but it was no use. He couldn't for the life of him remember where he was on that one night, six months earlier.

TAKE ME BACK TO THE BALL GAME

J uan had been sitting in limbo for months when during a phone call, Alma told him that she had been going over it in her mind and she thought that he might have been at the Dodgers game on the night in question, with six-year-old Melissa. When she said that, memories of the game came flooding back. Juan had trouble remembering a lot of things, but he remembered every detail of every ball game he had ever gone to. He didn't remember what happened that night, but he could give a blow-by-blow description of the game. It had been a tie coming in to the ninth, but the Dodgers had lost 11-4.

Juan was sure the tickets were somewhere in his home. He was a hoarder and liked to keep memorabilia and souvenirs of the games he went to, and he had better seats than usual at this particular one. Alma looked everywhere Juan thought they could be, but she had no luck.

Grasping at this lifeline, Todd told Alma to turn the

entire apartment upside down if necessary. She had to do
anything she could to find those tickets, and once she
found them, she wasn't to touch them. So that's what
Alma did. Sure enough, tucked away in a dresser drawer,
were two tickets to the Dodgers vs Braves game at Dodger
Stadium on May 12, 2003.

Juan was overjoyed, but Todd warned him that the
tickets alone would not be enough. All they proved was
that *somebody* had been at the game that night, but not
necessarily Juan. Juan's cousin and friend who had been
at the ball game that day were not considered reliable
witnesses for the defense.

What the tickets did show were the seat numbers that
Juan and his daughter sat in. Todd thought he might be
able to find some clues there, and organised a meeting at
the stadium with Sam Fernandez, Senior Vice President
and General Counsel for the Dodgers. Sam was
extremely helpful and allowed Todd to go to where the
seats were and take photographs from all angles, so he
would know exactly what he was looking for in the next
step. Todd had heard of DodgerCam, which constantly
panned the crowd. He requested all of the footage shot on
that night. Then he sat in front of a video, slowing down
to view it frame by frame whenever the camera panned to
the stand where Juan's seats were.

He was able to identify the seats and that there were
people in them. Todd was sure it was Juan and his daughter, but the video was too blurry to make a positive identification. They could have been anyone.

When Todd told Juan the news, Juan suddenly
remembered something else from that night. He told his
lawyer about being blocked from returning to his seat by

a TV camera. It wasn't a normal game camera, it was something different. All he remembered were security personnel blocking the aisle, and a bald white guy walking up and down the stairs, and then Juan and Melissa being ushered through, which meant they had walked in front of the camera. Could that camera possibly have caught him on film?

Todd went back to the Dodgers and asked for their help to identify what the camera crew was filming. The stadium did allow filming from time to time, but it was rare for filming to take part during an actual game. Film crews were not supposed to inconvenience the paying fans. Sam Fernandez agreed to open up his record books.

On May 12, there was just one entry in the book. HBO had been filming an episode of their hit comedy series, *Curb Your Enthusiasm*.

CURB YOUR ENTHUSIASM

Curb Your Enthusiasm is a high-budget, high-quality comedy series produced by and starring Larry David. Larry plays a fictionalized version of himself, going about his daily life, with all his neuroses and quirks exaggerated for comedic effect. He is best known as the creator of *Seinfeld* and is one of the most powerful men in Hollywood. The *Seinfeld* character of George Costanza was rumored to be loosely based on Larry.

When Todd contacted HBO to request to view the footage from Dodger Stadium, he met with reluctance. The episode that was being shot that day had not yet aired, and HBO was strict about letting pre-production footage be seen by anyone. What's more, there were 56,000 people at the game and only two cameras. The chances of this one guy being on camera were astronomically small.

Mustering up every ounce of his charm, Todd described the most unusual situation that had arisen in regard to Juan Catalan. He impressed on the executives that viewing that footage was quite literally a matter of life or death. Todd was absolutely sure that his client was innocent, but without an alibi, he could be facing the death penalty. He was so passionate and convincing that his request was put through to Larry David himself.

Todd's ardent entreaties worked, and Larry gave the go-ahead, noting that the story was so bizarre it could have been a script for an episode of his show. Todd went into the studio in Santa Monica and was put into an editing room with permission to go through all the rough tapes for the seventh episode of season four of *Curb Your Enthusiasm*.

The episode was called "The Car Pool Lane." In it, Larry is in a hurry to get to a Dodgers game, so he hires a sex worker to sit with him in the car so that he can use the car pool lane on the highway. She ends up accompanying him to the stadium, where he is upset at what he considers lousy seats. There is a scene where Larry briefly walks down the aisle to try and sit next to his friend Marty Funkhouser, who is sitting in a field-level seat. He is made to return to the lousy seats, much to his annoyance.

In a painfully ironic scene, Larry's friend Marty gets arrested for a crime he didn't commit, when holding a jacket with medicinal marijuana in it while Larry goes to the bathroom.

Todd Melnik watched the episode and recognized the stand where Juan and his daughter had been seated, but there was no sign of his client. He then went through every bit of outtake footage that had been shot that day.

He was on the fifth or sixth tape, and he couldn't

believe his eyes. The camera was shooting down the aisle as Larry David walked up from the front-row seats. In HBO high resolution, a man in a white Dodgers T-shirt with number 27 on the back and holding the hand of a little girl walked into the shot, apparently oblivious to the fact that he was about to cut off the star of the show. When the man turned to take his seat, his face was shown as clear as day. There was no doubt it was Juan Catalan.

Todd Melnik sat back in disbelief. It confirmed what he knew in his heart to be true. His client was innocent and now he had an alibi to prove it.

When Todd called Juan with the news, Juan was elated. He had been wasting away in prison for nearly six months, the threat of death row forever looming over him. He knew that the odds were stacked against a lower socioeconomic Latino man from a family with gang affiliations. He could not depend on an acquittal based on due process of the legal system. He desperately needed that alibi.

Todd and Juan's elation proved to be premature. The time stamp on the tape featuring Juan was 9.15 p.m. Martha was shot at 10.32 p.m. The prosecution said it would have been plausible for Juan to have left the stadium before the game ended and made it to Martha's address in time to carry out the shooting. What's more, by Juan's own admission and confirmed by his own witnesses, he had been on Martha's street at 10.43 p.m. that night, dropping off his cousin Miguel, just 150 yards away from where Martha lay dead. The evidence they believed was going to exonerate Juan was declared effectively useless. Juan was not going to be allowed out of prison on the basis of the HBO outtake footage.

Todd asked Juan to try and recall anything at all that might put him at the stadium for another hour. Juan's insistence that there was no way he was leaving the game when it was a 4–4 tie going into the ninth wasn't enough. Juan recalled buying souvenir cards at the end of the night, after the game had finished. He had looked through them for a while, but he had bought them with cash. There was no credit card record of the purchase.

Todd asked Juan for his phone and noted a very brief incoming call at 10.11 p.m on the night of the game. The call was from Alma, no doubt asking Juan what time he expected to be home. It only lasted forty-nine seconds.

Todd had been present at the O.J. Simpson trial a few years earlier and recalled a technique that had been used in that trial to place O.J. during the slow speed car chase. Police were able to find out which cell towers his phone was pinging off when a call was transmitted. Todd set about getting a subpoena for the telephone records for that night. The records confirmed that Juan's phone had been inside Dodger Stadium when he took that call.

JUAN'S ALIBI

At Juan's preliminary hearing, a judge had to decide whether to send Juan for jury trial where he could be sentenced to death, or dismiss the charges altogether. Todd Melnik painstakingly went through all of the evidence that placed Juan at Dodger Stadium at the time of Martha's murder. The judge listened to the tape of Juan's interrogation over and over the night before, trying to decide if he sounded like a guilty man.

Little Melissa was called to the stand. She said she had been at the Dodger's game with daddy and she remembered getting ice-cream and Dodgers cards. Todd pointed out the discrepancies in the witness's original statement. The witness said the gunman had a goatee, which Juan never had, and that he was a stocky 5'8" or 5'10". Juan was lean and tall, at 6'1". Todd played the tapes of Juan's interrogation, in which he never wavered in his protestations of innocence and pleaded to be allowed to take a lie detector test.

Todd had warned him that, whatever he heard in the courtroom, he was to remain calm and never lash out. Juan was severely tested when the police eyewitness, who gave the description that the composite sketch was drawn, was called to testify. When the prosecutor asked if he could see the shooter in the courthouse, the man pointed at Juan, who just shook his head, but remained quiet.

Juan stayed shackled to his chair, squirming uncomfortably and trying not to look at Martha's family who were once again in court to watch the proceedings and see justice done for their daughter.

When the judge began to speak, she spoke of the prosecution's star witness, whom she described as credible and honest, with no incentive to lie. However, it was dark, he was panicked and in an extremely stressful situation and under a cloud of suspicion himself. With the video and phone tower evidence, taking into consideration the traffic of the evening, the judge acknowledged it would have been nearly impossible for Juan to have made it to Martha's house in time to shoot her. He could not, in all fairness, be committed to stand trial for a crime that carried the death penalty.

Juan didn't understand what she was saying, until Todd turned to him and told him it was over. He was free.

Juan was released straight into the arms of Alma and his two daughters, a reunion that was caught by TV cameras. He had lost thirty pounds while he was in prison and all he wanted was a can of Coke. It had been six months since he had had any sort of soda. First, he turned to Todd and gave him one last hug. Then Juan and his family went to buy that Coke.

The next day he went and bought a box set of *Curb Your Enthusiasm*.

JUST A RUSE

Although this was a wonderful outcome for Juan Catalan, it was devastating for Martha's parents. Speaking no English, they relied on the police to let them know what was going on. The police had assured them that they had caught their daughter's murderer and that he would pay for his crime.

They didn't understand why Juan had been released. Juan had been positively identified by a witness; his face picked out of a lineup. They thought he must have been let off on a technicality, or by the work of a clever lawyer.

A few days later, Juan's cousin came back from the machine shop where Juan worked with his father with a story to tell. Martha's mother had been standing outside, behaving erratically and screaming for Juan to come out and get what he deserved. Juan's cousin was worried she was mentally unhinged. She had screamed and cried and hid in the bushes outside the factory where she thought Juan was working.

In 2004, suffering from post-traumatic stress disorder,

Juan Catalan sued the City of Los Angeles, the police department and four detectives, including detectives Pinner and Rodriguez. He wanted compensation for the stress and anguish of being arrested at gunpoint in front of his four-year-old daughter, wrongly accused of murder and placed on what was essentially death row for six months.

Under cross-examination, Pinner and Rodriguez admitted to fabricating evidence against Juan, including circling his name on a six pack and forging the words and signature of the supposed witness. They justified their actions, calling it a "ruse" that they used to elicit a confession.

It was exactly the same "ruse" they had used on Jose Ledesma, when they claimed Martha had identified him for the murder of Christian Vargas. A ruse that Martha's parents were still unaware of.

Juan's case was drawn out, as such cases for civil damages usually are. In the meantime, detectives Pinner and Rodriguez remained on the Homicide Squad and Martha Puebla's murder remained technically an open case. Nobody seemed to be doing much about it though, as police still believed they had let the murderer slip through their fingers. There was nobody else to look for.

Later that year, a new break came in Martha's case. Federal investigators got involved in the investigation as part of a larger case against the Vineland Boyz. Vineland members had shot and murdered Burbank police officer Matthew Pavelka and wounded and paralyzed his partner in November 2003. One gang member was killed during the shoot-out. The murder of a police officer was the final straw, and the authorities set to work dismantling the Vineland Boyz.

During January 2005, prosecutors started preparations for Jose Ledesma's trial for the murder of Christian Vargas. When reviewing evidence, they came across recordings of the telephone calls Jose has made from prison. They had been badly transcribed and didn't make much sense. Spanish-speaking LAPD officers listened to the recording and heard Jose Ledesma giving an order to kill Martha Puebla to somebody called "Cokester." There was another call to Cokester two weeks later, on May 30, 2003, about another witness, another teenage girl. Using coded language, Jose told Cokester that he needed to kill another teenage girl, Teresa Mendez.

Cokester was quickly identified as gang member and Jose's friend, Javier Covarrubias. The order to kill Martha Puebla by a member of one of the most dangerous gangs in Los Angeles had been recorded, but nobody had bothered to listen to it and Martha Puebla had never gone into witness protection.

In June 2005, a task force was formed comprising 1,300 officers and agents from six local police agencies, FBI, DEA, U.S. Marshals Service and the Internal Revenue Service. They conducted Operation Silent Night, with the Vineland Boyz gang squarely in their sights.

JUSTICE DENIED

I n March 2007, Juan Catalan was awarded $320,000 in a settlement of his lawsuit against the City of Los Angeles. The case had dragged on for over three years.

Although his payout for wrongful imprisonment was woefully inadequate for what he was subjected to, the court found that the detectives had probable cause for making the arrest and had acted in good faith when they doctored the six pack to make it look like a witness had picked Juan out of a lineup. Juan could have fought it out in front of a jury, but there was a good chance he would have wound up with nothing at all.

IN JANUARY 2008, nearly five years after Martha Puebla's murder, Jose Ledesma, in a plea bargain struck with the city to avoid the death penalty, confessed to the murders of Enrique Acosta and Christian Vargas, and to soliciting the murders of both Martha Puebla and Teresa Mendez.

Vineland Boyz gang members Javier Covarrubius (aka Cokester), Raul Robledo, and Luis Sandoval pleaded guilty to locating and killing Martha Puebla under the instructions of Jose Ledesma. Raul Robledo was the gunman who shot teenage Martha in the face.

It was in court in 2008, with the assistance of a translator, that Martha's parents heard for the first time about the role that detectives Pinner and Rodriguez had played in Martha's death. They had no idea that Martha had been falsely labelled an informant by the detectives, nor that Jose Ledesma had ordered her murder from prison. Her parents stated that neither they nor Martha had been offered any sort of protection. It was only after Martha's death that her parents had been moved to another state for their own safety. They had relied on the police chief and the City of Los Angeles for all information about the investigations into the murder. The police somehow forgot to tell them about their "ruse" and Martha's parents remained in the dark.

On May 13, 2008, lawyers acting on behalf of Martha Rauda and Regulo Puebla filed a complaint for damages against the City of Los Angeles, Chief William Bratton, Detective Martin Pinner and Detective Juan Rodriguez. The suit claimed that the detectives had falsely and knowingly informed a murder suspect and gang member that Martha had identified him as a shooter in a gang murder, and that Martha's murder was a foreseeable result of their actions. They believed the failure to tell them was deliberate.

Once again, the proceedings were drawn out for years. A slew of lawyers worked on the wrongful death lawsuit for Martha Puebla's parents on a "no-win, no-fee" basis.

Police claimed that Martha and her family had been offered protection, something Martha's parents denied. One officer testified that he had heard that protection had been offered but had not been at the meeting where that was told to Martha or her parents. During discovery, a detailed log the detectives kept of their investigation showed no indication that they had contact with Martha or her parents after they used Martha to bait Jose during the interrogation. The tactic itself was deemed acceptable practice. The detectives blamed a poor transcription service for not being aware of the phone call Jose placed to put out a hit on Martha.

The family's lawyer told the court, "Martha Puebla was murdered because the LAPD put a bull's-eye on her back by telling a gang member that she was a snitch."

In return, the lawyer representing the city and LAPD said that it was Martha's testimony at Jose's preliminary hearing, not the detectives' interrogation, that led to her murder. Even though she had not identified Jose as the killer, she had testified to other information, such as his gang affiliation, and that would have been enough for the gang to seek retaliation.

In April 2010, following a trial, a jury found detectives Martin Pinner and Juan Rodriguez acted maliciously and recklessly and had violated the due process rights of Martha and her parents; that they had acted negligently; that their negligence was a substantial contributing factor in Martha's death; and that they had acted with reckless disregard for the rights of Martha and/or her parents.

But the jury also found that sixteen-year-old Martha and/or her parents had acted negligently and that this negligence was a substantial factor in causing Martha's death. They somehow apportioned 20% of the responsibility for Martha's death to the detectives, with the remaining 80% to Martha herself and/or her parents.

Martha's parents were awarded a grand total of $1 for the wrongful death of their daughter. But at least the lawyers got paid, with the court awarding attorney fees and costs of approximately $730,000.

Both detectives Pinner and Rodriguez remained in the LAPD, although Martin Pinner was finally removed from the Homicide Squad and reassigned to cases involving juveniles in July 2008. Detective Rodriguez had already been transferred to auto fraud in 2004 but by July 2008 he was working in the vice unit.

The taskforce assigned to dismantle the Vineyard Boyz "Operation Silent Night" resulted in twenty-three arrests of gang members. In February 2019, nearly forty members were arrested in another raid on the gang.

Lying to suspects in order to elicit a confession remains a permissible tactic for police, but after a series of articles in the *Los Angeles Times*, the LAPD announced changes to training to make clear to detectives that they must weigh the benefit of lying to a suspect against the potential danger the lies may create. They were also to be told that they have an obligation to offer police protection to someone they believe they have placed in danger. The articles also seemed to be the catalyst for taking Martin Pinner off homicide cases.

The one good thing to come out of the whole sorry mess was that Juan Catalan's life turned around. He used his compensation payout wisely. He went to college, got an associate's degree and worked toward his bachelor's degree. He went to underprivileged schools to speak to students about the importance of their education and told them that their past circumstances and upbringing did not have to determine their future.

He visits Mario in prison and puts money on "his books"—the account prisoners can use to buy themselves certain permitted items, like candy bars and soda—but he is determined he will never see the inside of a prison as an inmate again.

He has not been able to speak with Martha's family, but feels no ill will toward them. Like him, they were also victims of the LAPD. He told the *What's Up Fool* podcast, "I feel for the family man, they lost their daughter, they tried to sue the LAPD and they got $1. One dollar, bro, what kind of slap in the face is that?"

In 2019, Netflix released a documentary about Juan's ordeal called *Long Shot*. Juan had been reluctant to take part initially, but he agreed to do it as a favor to Todd Melnik, the attorney who had gone above and beyond in finding the evidence that was used to exonerate him and whom Juan refers to as his "White Knight." The documentary received great reviews and has led to even more opportunities for Juan, who now always gets the good seats at Dodgers games. He tells his daughters they can grow up and do anything, be anyone they want to be.

As for his own ordeal, Juan, like his mother, firmly

believes everything happens for a reason. He told the *What's Up Fool* podcast that his life had done a full 180 and that it was all for the better. He said, "Sometimes God has to throw a brick at us to get our attention, man, and that definitely got my attention."

ALSO BY EILEEN ORMSBY

Psycho.com (Dark Webs Book 1)

Murder on the Dark Web (Dark Webs Book 2)

Stalkers (Dark Webs Book 3)

The Darkest Web

Silk Road

Blue Skies, Black Death (short)

Keep going for sneak peeks of these books

PLEA FROM THE AUTHOR

Hey, True Crime fan,

So you got to the end of my book. I hope that means that you enjoyed it or learned something from it. Regardless, I would just like to thank you for giving me your valuable time to share these stories with you.

I am truly blessed to have such a fulfilling job, but I only have that job because of people like you; people kind enough to give my books a chance and spend their hard earned money buying them. For that I am eternally grateful.

If you enjoyed this book and would like to help, then you could think about leaving a review on Amazon, Goodreads, or anywhere else that readers visit.

The most important part of how well a book sells is how many positive reviews it has, so if you leave me one then you are directly helping me to continue writing these books. Thank you in advance to anyone who does.

DARK WEBS BOOK 1
PSYCHO.COM

Serial killers have been with us for decades. The internet has put them in our pockets.

A pair of teens go on a murderous rampage and their exploits are immortalised in the most shocking video ever to circulate the internet, "3 Guys, 1 Hammer"

A serial killer with over 100 kills to his name walks free and becomes a Youtube sensation

A psychopath lures victims through online dating to use as "research" for his twisted film project

Psycho.com is a chilling look at what happens when murderous minds meet modern technology.

Buy Psycho.com on Kindle

Or download the entire collection of books 1-3 here for a great discount!

DARK WEBS BOOK 2
MURDER ON THE DARK WEB

A look into the dark side of the internet's secret underbelly

The dark web is the internet's evil twin, where anything can be bought and sold. Drugs, weapons, and hackers-for-hire are available at the touch of a button.

Most who visit merely look around, happy to simply satisfy their curiosity before leaving, never to return. But some are sucked into the criminal underworld and find themselves doing things they would never have contemplated in the real world—ordering a hit on a love rival or bidding on an auction for a sex slave - like the people in this book.

A Minnesota dog trainer is found dead of an apparent suicide after detectives find her details on a dark web murder-for-hire site. But who paid $13,000 in Bitcoin to kill this devout Christian and beloved wife and mother?

A Page-3 glamour model is drugged, kidnapped and listed for sale on a dark web human trafficking site. A secret society called Black Death demands a ransom for her safe return, or else she will be sold to sadistic millionaires to use before feeding to the tigers.

These are extraordinary true tales of infidelity, betrayal and shadowy hitmen and human traffickers who may not be that they seem.

Note: This is a standalone book in the Dark Webs True Crime series. It is not necessary to have read the others in the series

Download Murder on the Dark Web for Kindle here

Or download the entire collection of books 1-3 here for a great discount!

DARK WEBS BOOK 3
STALKERS

Deluded narcissists. Obsessed fans. Sinister internet trolls.

Stalkers who turned deadly

A Hollywood starlet on a smash-hit sitcom is unaware that her greatest fan is hell-bent on meeting his crush

A gameshow winner is determined to make the object of his affections love him back

A teenaged boy is convinced he is a spy with a licence to kill

A Craigslist ad for a fantasy roleplay is not what it seems

Dark Webs Book 3 takes you into the twisted world of stalkers and the devastating impact their obsessions can have on their victims.

Note: This is a standalone book in the Dark Webs True Crime series. It is not necessary to have read the others in the series

Download Stalkers for Kindle here

Or download the entire collection of books 1-3 here for a great discount!

THE DARKEST WEB

The Darkest Web

Dark...

A kingpin willing to murder to protect his dark web drug empire. A corrupt government official determined to avoid exposure. The death of a dark web drugs czar in mysterious circumstances in a Bangkok jail cell, just as the author arrives there.

Who is Variety Jones and why have darknet markets ballooned tenfold since authorities shut down the original dark web drugs bazaar, Silk Road? Who are the kingpins willing to sell poisons and weapons, identities and bank accounts, malware and life-ruining services online to anyone with a wallet full of Bitcoin?

Darker...

A death in Minnesota leads detectives into the world of dark web murder-for-hire where hundreds of thousands of dollars in Bitcoin is paid to arrange killings, beatings and rapes. Meanwhile, the owner of the most successful hitman website in history is threatening the journalists who investigate his business with a visit from his operatives - and the author is at the top of his list.

Darkest...

People with the most depraved perversions gather to share their obscene materials in an almost inaccessible corner of the dark web. A video circulates and the pursuit of the monsters responsible for 'Daisy's Destruction' lead detectives into the unimaginable horror of the world of hurtcore.

There's the world wide web - the internet we all know that connects us via news, email, forums, shopping and social media. Then there's the dark web - the parallel internet accessed by only a select few. Usually, those it connects wish to remain anonymous and for good reason.

Eileen Ormsby has spent the past five years exploring every corner of the Dark Web. She has shopped on darknet markets, contributed to forums, waited in red rooms and been threatened by hitmen on murder-for-hire sites. On occasions, her dark web activities have poured out into the real world and she has attended trials, met with criminals and the law enforcement who tracked them down, interviewed dark web identities and visited them in prison.

This book will take you into the murkiest depths of the web's dark underbelly: a place of hitmen for hire, red rooms, hurtcore sites and markets that will sell anything a person is willing to pay for - including another person. The Darkest Web.

Published by Allen & Unwin

Download The Darkest Web for Kindle

SILK ROAD

It was the 'eBay of drugs', a billion dollar empire. Behind it was the FBI's Most Wanted Man, a mysterious crime czar dubbed 'Dread Pirate Roberts'. SILK ROAD lay at the heart of the 'Dark Web' - a parallel internet of porn, guns, assassins and drugs. Lots of drugs. With the click of a button LSD, heroin, meth, coke, any illegal drug imaginable, would wing its way by regular post from any dealer to any user in the world. How was this online drug cartel even possible? And who was the mastermind all its low roads led to? This is the incredible true story of Silk Road's rise and fall, told with unparalleled insight into the main players - including alleged founder and kingpin Dread Pirate Roberts himself - by lawyer and investigative journalist Eileen Ormsby. A stunning crime story with a truth that explodes off the page.

Published by Pan MacMillan

Download Silk Road for Kindle

REFERENCES AND
ACKNOWLEDGMENTS

Once again, I have to thank my friend and legendary editor Lorna Hendry for all that she does to make my words more consistent and readable.

Thanks to retired detective Richard Graham for providing an extensive interview of his experience investigating the death of Shauna Howe.

As always, as well as parliamentary committee reports, court documents and records, I consulted hundreds of news articles, TV episodes and documentaries - too many to possibly list them all. As a general rule, if there was an article, podcast or documentary about it, I read, listened to or watched it. Below is a selection of some publications that were of significance to the final product

In particular, I want to draw attention to the work of Kerry Carrington and her large volume of work in regard to the assault and murder of Leigh Leigh

ABC Background Briefing, *Sticks and Stones: the Killing of Leigh Leigh* Broadcast: Sun 29 Sep 1996

Byrne-Armstrong, Hilary, Moira Carmody, Bob Hodge, Russell Hogg & Murray Lee (1999) "The Risk of Naming Violence: An Unpleasant Encounter Between Legal Culture and Feminist Criminology", Australian Feminist Law Journal, 13:1, 13-37

Carrington, Kerry (1998) *Who killed Leigh Leigh? A story of shame and mateship in an Australian town* Random House Australia

Carrington, K., & Johnson, A. (1995). Some Justice for Leigh Leigh. Australian Feminist Law Journal, 5(1), 126–132.

Chan, H. C. (2019). *A Global Casebook of Sexual Homicide.*

Heide, Kathleen M., Eric Beauregard & Wade C. Myers (2009) Sexually Motivated Child Abduction Murders: Synthesis of the Literature and Case Illustration, Victims & Offenders: An International Journal of Evidence-based Research, Policy, and Practice, 4:1, 58-75

Morrow, Jonathan; Roque, Mehera San --- "In Her Death She Remains as the Limit of the System: Notes Towards an Ethical Writing of Collective Sexual Violence" [1996] SydLawRw 28; (1996) 18(4) Sydney Law Review 474

Mouzos, Jenny, *Homicidal encounters: a study of homicide in Australia 1989–1999* Australian Institute of Criminology June 2000

The Lake Eirie Murders S2 E1 - "Devil at the Crossroads" Discovery Communications 2020

Long Shot, Netflix documentary 2019

Printed in Great Britain
by Amazon

59483591R00173